AMIGO É COISA PARA SE GUARDAR
DO LADO ESQUERDO DO PEITO.
ASSIM FALAVA A CANÇÃO DA AMERICA.

MILTON NASCIMENTO

A friend is something that one
should treasure on the left side of
one's breast. That's how a *Song from
America* put it.

MRP

KARIN STURM

AYRTON SENNA

GOODBYE CHAMPION, FAREWELL FRIEND

Foreword by GERHARD BERGER

Motor Racing Publications

Contents

Foreword

by Gerhard Berger

I'm quite sure that every budding racing driver considers himself the greatest of all time and thinks to himself: if only I could be behind the wheel of the right car, they wouldn't see me for dust.

I wasn't any different.

But in spring 1983 my view of the world was thoroughly shaken. At a Formula 3 European Championship race at Silverstone I came across Ayrton Senna for the first time. It had been raining, and in the wet I was always damned fast. I'd heard of Senna as the absolute ace, the best thing that had ever reached us from Brazil, who left everyone standing. I drove to the limit and beyond; I couldn't go any faster. After practice, not only was Senna ahead of me, I was 4 seconds slower; then I realized that one could go faster... I had a healthy respect for the guy from the beginning.

I liked him from the first, and evidently he liked me too, but that didn't stop us from driving into each other's cars at the beginning of a Brazilian Grand Prix. That incident told us both something very clearly: that the other person was not one who was in the habit of giving way. That our growing friendship not only survived the three years together with the McLaren team, but really developed during that time, is perhaps incomprehensible for many. In Formula 1 your team-mate is supposed to be your greatest enemy, the one whose weaknesses you have to exploit, the one you must hate. I couldn't do that. I probed Ayrton more than anybody else, I tried to get to the bottom of him, to fathom his secret and to learn from him. And the result of all this was his only really close friendship in Formula 1, and mine.

In speed, reflexes, eyes and courage he had no advantage over me; that was shown by the McLaren computer print-outs. From our first practice together we pushed each other to new limits. He drove his best time, then I went out and drove an even quicker time. As the mechanics pushed me back into the pits I looked across to him. He flashed a glance at me through the slit in his visor as if to say: "You lunatic, now I've got to go out again!"

After the practice he came to me with the computer print-out in his hand and pointed to a straight line which meant that I had gone flat-out round the bend, and he said to me: "You're crazy, if you go off the track there you've had it!"

He wasn't absolutely fearless. He was a gifted racing driver with the greatest degree of perfection and concentration, combining common-sense, concentration, power and speed with a talent for driving and the capacity not to make mistakes at critical moments. He had an absolute overview, he knew everything, he could do everything. He was simply two or three levels above the rest of us. Somebody who didn't work with him and know him so well may not be willing to believe that. Of course, there are still lots of people in Formula 1 who believe they could have beaten Senna. I can only say: the poor guys have no idea how far away from him they are. I am glad that I had the chance to get to know him well enough to be able to judge it.

By nature, Senna was an extremely hardworking and ambitious fellow. That, and his extraordinary ability, perhaps made him unapproachable for many: a supernatural being whom one can't relate to. But in the course of time he became more relaxed. A warm sense of fun developed between us, which really suited him. I'm sure Karin Sturm will write in this book about some of the tricks we played on each other - she was one of the few to whom Ayrton opened his heart, and sometimes poured out his troubles, for example when several dozen frogs were jumping all over his hotel room!

Josef Leberer, one of the most important people in Ayrton's life, told me a story about the start at Imola. The announcer was giving the starting positions; there was applause for Senna, and then louder applause for Berger, of course on account of Ferrari. The special applause for me had really amused Senna; according to Josef he grinned from ear to ear. So, as I remember Ayrton Senna I will imagine this grin, perhaps his last expression of warmheartedness before the accident.

He taught me a lot about our sport; I taught him to laugh.

Gerhard Berger

Imola – whom the gods love...

Diary of the last weekend

May 1 in Imola is fine and warm, no longer spring-like, almost a summer day. The evening is still warm, even though the sun has already disappeared behind the trees at the Tamburello bend. The icy cold comes from within, from the encounter with reality.

The marks on the asphalt and on the concrete wall tell a clear, hard, brutal story. They destroy the last illusion that one can wake up from the nightmare. Nevertheless, the stillness, the bewilderment, the dignity of the few people who have gathered here all make the cold a little more bearable... There are a few flowers by the wall, then a photograph, the first letters and greetings, on whatever slip or scrap of paper that came to hand, the last farewell to a racing driver, an idol – and a friend.

Imola, Sunday evening, May 1. It's quite dark now. The first stars shine dimly through the tears, and the blurred thoughts gradually get clearer and sharper, going back to

Crossing the finishing line at Imola for the last time, on Sunday, May 1, 1994 at 2.17pm: Ayrton Senna in the Williams-Renault is leading Michael Schumacher, his great rival of 1994.

the beginning of what still seems unreal and incomprehensible...

The fatal Imola weekend began for Ayrton Senna on Thursday at the Sheraton Hotel in Padua with a press conference to present his new mountain bike, a joint project with the Italian Carraro company. It's something that has been planned for a long time, one of the many new products under the famous 'Red S' Senna brand name. There are hardly any Formula 1 journalists, mostly local dignitaries from Padua and the immediate area. But what strikes the few experts there is that Senna, especially at the beginning of the event, is unusually tense, he seems nervous and strained. He relaxes only gradually and then tries to radiate confidence: "The World Championship is just beginning for me in Imola, with a handicap of two races," he comments.

In Padua there is a lot of private discussion about the rumours as to whether Benetton as well as Ferrari has been racing – and perhaps is still racing – using the banned traction control on their cars. Does part of the pressure on him come from anxiety about facing unfair competition?

"I really can't say much about it," he comments carefully, and then answers, in a way that says both very little and yet a lot: "It's difficult to talk about things one cannot prove."

On Friday morning he is well satisfied with the Williams, which has been aerodynamically remodelled; in the afternoon there is the shock of Rubens Barrichello's accident – he flew off at the third chicane over the kerbstones, cleared the tyre barrier, bounced back off the fence and ended up suspended unconscious in his car. Immediately after the accident nobody dared to believe that Rubens had got away with a broken nose and bruised ribs.

Senna is very concerned; he's worried about Barrichello and pays him a quick visit in the racetrack's medical centre. When the interrupted practice begins again he improves on his initial time by almost a second and finishes with a lead of about half a second – but he is shattered. As he climbs out of the car and leaves the pits he wants to start his usual round of interviews, but he is visibly irritated. He is put off as well by a few fans who vociferously greet him from the balcony above the Williams transporter, trying to encourage him with shouts of "Now's your chance to show Schumacher who's the champion" and similar. Senna is obviously unable to ignore them as he usually does.

When RTL reporter Kai Ebel asks him about Rubens Barrichello he begins a sentence three times, but keeps on losing the thread of his thoughts. "Sorry, I can't manage. Give me a bit of time to calm down," he blurts out and hurries into the transporter...

When he comes out half an hour later, he's pulled himself together: "It was a really weird practice today, Rubens' accident created bad feelings from the start. He's a friend of mine – afterwards I didn't manage a single decent lap without mistakes," he admits. "The car was OK, even if I can't say much about it due to the quite peculiar circumstances – the conditions have been constantly changing. But today I wasn't perfect."

And then he adds to the Italians that Imola is a dangerous circuit; there are a few places "which are not right as far as safety is concerned. But there are other circuits like that..." And why haven't the drivers done anything about it? His answer sounds somehow resigned: "I am the only World Champion left – and I have opened my big mouth too often.

Over the years I have learnt that it's better to keep my head down..."

Late in the afternoon he gives a short exclusive interview to Brazilian journalist Mario Andrade e Silva, very much on the spur of the moment in a short break in the team briefing, while his race engineer David Brown goes off for a few minutes to get some new data.

Mario remembers: "It was only about his mountain bike presentation, because I couldn't be in Padua. We had made an appointment, but he had put it off twice; then he called me in and said either we do it quickly now, while David's away – 'or we'll not have another chance...' And that's how it was. As soon as David came back he immersed himself again in minute technical details with him... It was after 6 o'clock and I had the feeling that they were not even halfway through their briefing."

Senna indeed stays at the track till 8 o'clock in the evening, working incredibly intensively. He knows for sure: Imola has got to be the turning point in the World Championship. On Saturday morning Rubens Barrichello comes back to the track from the hospital. His teeth look a bit battered, his nose is swollen, his right arm is bandaged – "but nothing's broken", he says, smiling, but adds thoughtfully: "I know how lucky I am. I'm glad to be alive..." And he gives special thanks to Senna: "He's a real friend. It was great the way he showed concern for me, he inquired again on Friday evening how I was..."

On Saturday, disaster strikes for the first time. When the front wing breaks away from Roland Ratzenberger's Simtek at 314.9km/h (according to the last photo-electric measurement) on the Villeneuve bend, the Austrian doesn't stand a chance. The

The Padua presentation: Senna unveils his latest business project - his own mountain bike!

television pictures are brutal and leave no room for hope at all. Formula 1 holds its breath. Many people just creep away, but Senna seeks out direct confrontation with the hard reality – as he had in 1990 after Martin Donnelly's near-fatal accident in Spain, and again yesterday with Barrichello. He drives out to the scene of the accident in order to get a first-hand picture of

what happened, then goes to see Ratzenberger briefly before he is flown off by helicopter from the medical centre to Bologna.

As Ayrton comes back to the pits he looks shattered and goes straight into the transporter to change out of his racing clothes immediately. There's no thought of continuing to drive, even though Frank Williams asks him about it

shortly after: "But really more as a matter of form..."

Damon Hill doesn't want to continue either, nor do the drivers from Sauber and Benetton. Michael Schumacher is deeply affected and J.J. Lehto is crying: "I drove up here with Roland from Monaco."

Heinz-Harald Frentzen, who did a lot together with Ratzenberger in Japan, wants to go straight back to his hotel: "I don't want to have to talk with anyone."

Senna, too, seeks complete seclusion. He runs the few yards from the transporter to the caravan – with an indescribable look in his eyes, as though he is taking nothing in. Later we hear: "He hardly spoke with anybody all day." Obviously he wants to cope with his feelings alone.

He leaves shortly before 5.30pm and nobody dares to go near him – he still has this aura of absolute isolation and unapproachability about him.

At the evening meal he asks his Austrian fitness coach and friend Josef Leberer, who was celebrating his birthday that Saturday, about Ratzenberger. "Where he came from, what he was like, what kind of person. He had hardly known him..." Josef thought of getting hold of an Austrian flag: "If Ayrton goes onto the rostrum on Sunday, I thought to myself, I'll give it to him. He would surely have been glad to take it up with him in honour of Roland."

That night Senna also calls his girlfriend Adriane, who didn't come with him to Imola, and says: "I have a really bad feeling about this race, I would rather not drive..." Adriane's mother later made this comment public on Brazilian television.

As Senna arrives in the paddock at about 8.30 on Sunday morning he is still visibly strained, but by comparison with yesterday he is a little more open again; he takes in

Practice at Imola - the whole weekend the mood is quite strange, overshadowed by the accidents...

his surroundings and now and then greets people briefly... Niki Lauda speaks to him for at least 10 minutes, encouraging him to do something at last about safety, to take a lead among the drivers...

As he climbs into his car for the warm-up he seems very determined. The way he moves, gets into the car, drives off and comes back into the pits all gives the impression that he wants to transform the sorrow and rage which are still written on his face into a positive form of aggression. For the first time since Friday he is once more a second faster than the rest of the world.

During this half-hour his press spokeswoman Betise Assumpçao confirms a story that has been going the rounds as a rumour: Senna received a written warning on Saturday afternoon from the

Stewards of the Meeting. They said there was no reason for him to go to the scene of Roland Ratzenberger's accident, and that he should explain what he had intended. After all, he wasn't a safety official, it wasn't his job to worry about such matters... Betise's comments are quite acidic. "It's incredible. He even drove out there quite officially in a circuit safety vehicle... But they just want to intimidate him..." And then it slips out: "But it's like that the whole time. That suspended fine because of Irvine [to whom Senna had delivered a punch following an incident during the 1993 Japanese Grand Prix], they only did that because they wanted to put him under pressure, because they knew what he wanted to do about a drivers' trade union."

During the warm-up Senna sends

a short greeting over the Williams pit radio to Alain Prost, who was at his first Grand Prix of the year: "Hello, my friend, I've been missing you..."

The two old rivals also have a quick breakfast together this Sunday morning. Prost will later recall: "For the first time for a long time we had a really normal conversation, we set aside some differences that there were between us."

In the drivers' briefing Senna once again points out that the very slow formation lap behind a pace-car at Aida was absolute stupidity, "increased risk, too slow, as a result everybody's tyres and brakes were too cold at the start". He demands forcefully that it shouldn't happen in future. After the briefing he tries to arrange a discussion about safety with his colleagues, notably Michael Schumacher, Gerhard Berger and Michele Alboreto... They agree to hold a meeting on safety issues with all drivers in Monte Carlo on the Friday before the next race. There is no tension among the drivers. Michael Schumacher comments later: "I'm glad that we got closer again recently and that this last conversation also took place in a friendly atmosphere."

The recent search for harmony is in hindsight quite striking: since the Brazilian Grand Prix he has clearly been seeking contact again and again with Michael Schumacher and emphasizing that there was no hostility towards his great rival. On the way back from Aida, on the British Airways flight from Osaka to London on the Monday after the Pacific Grand Prix, he goes up to Mika Häkkinen and gives his former McLaren team-mate a friendly slap

At the scene of Roland Ratzenberger's ▷
accident: Senna wants to find out at
first hand, to know the truth.

on the shoulder, as if it were a cautious apology on his part. During the race on Sunday the Finn had rammed him hard at the first bend and Senna had understandably been very annoyed and had reacted snidely to Mika's offer of an apology, even to the extent of being somewhat abusive – and had then regretted it. The emotions are a recurring theme...

Also, a conversation we had early in March fits into this search for harmony. In Le Castellet, during a pause in testing at the Paul Ricard circuit, we were talking about 1984, his first year in Formula 1, and I mentioned to him that Johnny Cecotto, who was then his team-mate with Toleman, could still not forgive him that after his crash at Brands Hatch [during practice for the British Grand Prix, when Johnny suffered serious leg injuries] he had

never gone to see him. And Senna thought for a moment, as he so often did when an answer was important for him, and then said: "Yes, I can understand that from his point of view... It was a mistake on my part. I was terribly preoccupied after the crash, but I suppose I just didn't think that it would have made such a difference to Johnny if I had gone to see him... Sorry, but one doesn't get everything right."

The strange thing about this story is that on my way home from Le Castellet I happened to spot Johnny Cecotto on the plane from Marseilles to Munich, but unfortunately he was surrounded by a crowd of racing people so I had no opportunity then to tell him what Senna had said. Then about four months later – by this time Senna was dead, of course – I saw him again and this time he was

alone; he was very moved when I was able to tell him of Senna's apology...

Just before 1.30pm on May 1, before getting into his car for the last time, Ayrton Senna stands in the pits for a long time, gently leaning against the rear wing of the Williams, his gaze lost in the distance, emotions mirrored in his face. This isn't the normal phase of quiet concentration that we know so well. On the starting grid he takes his helmet off once more, something he does very rarely. Here again: emotions, strain, a lot of tension in his face. Not his usual self, somehow different – especially now, when we see the pictures. Only once, when his friend Gerhard Berger receives by far the most applause when he is introduced over the public address system, because he is a Ferrari driver, does he laugh warmly... Later, as Williams engineering director Patrick Head speaks briefly with him, there is once more a hint of a smile... But as he puts his helmet on for the last time the smile has long since gone.

He wins the start, then the pace-car intervenes because of the Lehto-Lamy collision on the starting grid [Lehto's car stalled and Lamy, unsighted, ran into the back of him]. Then, after four more slow laps, they're off again and the accident comes when he's still in the lead, intent on building an advantage on the way to what is so important and necessary for him: victory. Tamburello, a place of fate? It is 2.17pm when, on entering the gentle left bend, the Williams suddenly veers to the right and flies

David Coulthard

Williams-Renault test driver and Senna's replacement

The loss of Ayrton Senna is an unimaginable one, both to the sport and to anyone who knew him... Ayrton is irreplaceable. For lots of people who had him as a role model, it's a terrible shock because we all believed he was immortal, that if anyone was going to get killed it was not going to be Ayrton. And it will be a long time before anyone – even Michael Schumacher – can attain Ayrton's stature.

I'd only just begun to get to know Ayrton this year, when he joined the Williams team and I started to work with him as the test driver. He surprised me with his kindness and generosity. Ayrton's public image and the way he was when you met him were very different. To me he was a very shy person, but one who warmed to you very quickly. I'm just very sad that I wasn't able to develop my friendship with him a bit more, simply because of the fact that he was an extraordinary individual.

Ayrton did one thing for me that I found extremely touching. On the Sunday morning of the San Marino Grand Prix, while the team were busy at Imola and I was qualifying for the Formula 3000 race at Silverstone, I received a

fax from Williams. This was signed by almost everyone in the team, including a message from Ayrton. It said: "Very best to you, Ayrton Senna, '94." He didn't have to do that, but it showed that he cared. It was a very touching gesture which said a lot about the sort of person Ayrton was...

There are quite a few promising young drivers in Formula 1 now... but none of them can ever replace Ayrton Senna, one of the greatest motor racing champions there has ever been.

I will always remember him, and the brief, profound impact he had on my life. I'm sure countless people around the world feel the same.

The last few minutes before the start: ▷
only strain and emotion show on his face
– Ayrton Senna has never looked so tense
before a race.

straight into the wall; a brutal impact, then it bounces back and comes to rest at the trackside. Horror, followed by a moment of hope as the yellow helmet in the cockpit seems to move once more, then the slow realization of the probable reality. Doctors, blood, then the helicopter, the clinic in Bologna, the news of the serious head injuries, abruptly shattering the last illusions. In between, scraps of thoughts, memories of a very personal conversation in which he hinted that there were worse things for him than death, perhaps to have to vegetate with a severe disability, unable really to live any more.

The Maggiore hospital gives the official time of death as 6.40pm.

What remains is emptiness, questions and rage. Rage at the quite unpardonable tactlessness of FOCA head Bernie Ecclestone who, just 10 minutes after the accident, says coldly to Leonardo, Senna's younger brother: "I'm sorry, he's dead, but we'll only announce it after the end of the race", and then carries on calmly chewing an apple...

Bernie's later attempt to apologize, saying there had been a misunderstanding, a misheard radio message from the Grand Prix doctor Sid Watkins, whose "It's his head" became interpreted as "He is dead", sounds not only lame, but even more embarrassing because it seems not to have changed his basic attitude. The Senna family show style and consistency by later letting Ecclestone know that he would not be welcome at the funeral in São Paulo.

Inevitably, the question arises of

The brutal reality of the Tamburello bend: the doctors and helpers who are looking after Senna already sense that he has no chance; the head injuries are too severe.

the respect for human life of those responsible for allowing a race, marred such as this had been, to be allowed to continue, despite everything, to the bitter end; not only after it was known that Senna had no chance, but also after yet another accident, this time in the pits, in which four mechanics were injured. Whether the injured could be properly looked after there or not – the main thing, or so it would seem, is that the show must go on...

Then there's the question of the cause of the accident, and of the safety of cars today whose aerodynamics "don't work any more if a speck of dust gets on the wing", as Karl Wendlinger had put it so graphically in another context only two weeks earlier in Aida. The probability that something happened to the Williams immediately springs to mind. From Niki Lauda and Gerhard Berger to Jackie Stewart, the experts are agreed: "This is not a place where you get driver error. The bend is flat-out, you can't do anything wrong." Inevitably, there are several theories, but it begins to be questionable whether the precise cause will ever really be fully explained. Ligier design engineer Gerard Ducarouge has calculated: "If only a small part of the front wing breaks on the Tamburello bend at those speeds, with a g-force of 4.5, you instantly lose 500 kilos of downforce." That is a fundamental problem with modern racing cars.

During the week before Imola some misgivings were expressed within the Williams test team that under pressure from Benetton's successes in the first two races there was perhaps a little too much experimentation and improvization going on at the same time..." For Imola the front end of the Williams had been completely remodelled aerodynamically...

Back in England after the tragic race, Patrick Head is quoted as saying that the team could see from the telemetry recording that Senna had briefly eased his foot from the accelerator, which had probably made the vehicle unstable. This was interpreted by some as implying driver error, but Williams and Head later denied these comments forcefully – and in any case, on their own they would have been inconclusive.

Here, perhaps a quick refresher lesson in physics is in order: if you ease your foot from the accelerator there is a shift of weight forwards, as a result of which the car momentarily has more downforce at the front, and when something happens in that situation the tail is more likely to break away, but the car does not veer to the right on a left-hand bend.

Honda engineers who worked for a long time with Senna are convinced that "if he eased his foot from the accelerator it was because he had noticed that something was wrong with the car. He could feel the slightest thing, he was always like a living sensor."

They also believe that the violent bouncing of the Williams that had occurred several times during the previous lap – which is constantly mentioned and was put forward as a possible cause of the accident by Michael Schumacher, who was driving close behind Senna – was probably normal, something that had been clearly calculated: "Otherwise, Ayrton would have reacted, even if for example tyre damage was developing... Or if, because of the long time held up behind the pace-car, or perhaps because of a wrong tyre pressure, the car had sat differently... He was so sensitized to such things. He must have been suddenly surprised by something."

In Italy, people are producing photos and amateur films which supposedly indicate a defect in the suspension. Others believe it might have been the steering. Whatever one's suppositions, the big question which arises is: how safe or unsafe is the Imola track? Of course, one can't change everything everywhere

– but is it wise to have less than 10 metres of asphalt or grass as a safety zone and concrete walls at 300km/h bends? The argument that one wouldn't have expected an accident there because it was not a critical bend, as was put forward by Ferrari driver Nicola Larina after Roland Ratzenberger's accident, might have been valid for the Villeneuve bend, but surely not for Tamburello, site of the Senna accident, after the horrific crashes which had occurred there involving Nelson Piquet in '87, Gerhard Berger in '89 and Michele Alboreto during an earlier test-drive accident? So who shoulders the blame? Proceedings were opened against the circuit authorities at Imola – but the course was given a clean bill of health by Roland Bruynseraede, the FIA's head of safety. And the drivers themselves – including Senna – had never really protested, not least because they had been lulled into a false sense of security by years of good luck in Formula 1 during which there had been many accidents but not a single death...

But what remains above all, beyond all the questions, investigations and accusations, are the memories and the feelings. The crowds of people in Bologna on Monday and Tuesday, the sea of flowers and banners, the sorrow and bewilderment on so many faces, people's attempts to comfort one another, to help one another, to comprehend.

The worldwide reactions are remarkable, even in circles that usually have absolutely nothing to do with Formula 1; the shock is universal. "Since the murder of John F. Kennedy I cannot think of an occasion on which the death of one man has brought so much dismay," says journalist Dieter Stappert, who regularly followed Formula 1 many years ago...

Then there is the state funeral in São Paulo – not attended by Michael Schumacher, which is hard for people to understand, and not just in Brazil – the millions of people on the streets, the indescribable sorrow, a whole country weeping for its hero throughout the day, the government's demand for an official investigation into the circumstances of the accident.

Then the news that circles the globe: that Senna had made the street children of São Paulo the beneficiaries of his substantial life insurance policies. Those who knew him a bit better were not particularly surprised...

At the graveside, his sister Viviane says: "God gave Ayrton a mission. People don't care about each other any more, they live just for themselves. Especially here in Brazil. He united them – even through his death."

The family releases the news that everything that Ayrton has built up over the past few years alongside his racing career, the entire business enterprise, is to be continued in the spirit of his way of thinking by his father, his cousin Fabio Machado, who has already been business manager of Ayrton Senna Promoçoes in São Paulo, and by Julian Jakobi, who has been the head of the Senna office in London for two years. The Ayrton Senna Foundation will be established, and will receive a substantial share of the profits from his businesses – for charitable purposes.

The memory will live on... "In principle – though of course prematurely – he has achieved what he always wanted: immortality," says Gerd Krämer of Mercedes, one of Senna's closest friends. We called him "magic" – and the spell will not fade...

The red flag at Imola – the end of a dream, but only an interruption in the show which must go on...

The last winter, which was a summer

Happiness, hope and confidence

It was a favourite joke: Ayrton Senna was asked about his winter holiday in Brazil and he quipped: "Winter? You mean summer, don't you?" OK, winter in Europe is summer in Brazil!

The winter of 1993-94 brings him less holiday than usual, but it is still one of the happiest for him. With the Williams contract in his pocket, full of hope for a fantastic season, even the FIA with its suspended fine because of his attack on Eddie Irvine cannot destroy his peace. In the middle of December he comes to a go-kart meet at Bercy, in Paris, a charity event organized by Philippe Streiff, the French Formula 1 driver who has been a paraplegic since a test-drive accident in Brazil in 1989.

Senna takes a lot of trouble personally to smooth out a few differences between sponsors in order to make his participation at Bercy possible. There is a conflict between a contract with a petrol company made through McLaren which runs out at the end of the year and the main sponsor at Bercy. Finally they agree that he can drive in a neutral white kart.

During these two days in Paris he is relaxed in a way that has been rarely seen in public. With his girlfriend Adriane always beside him, he laughs that he had one of these special karts that are driven here sent to Brazil so that he could practice. "But unfortunately it arrived so late that I hardly had any time."

Naturally he is ambitious in this race – the desire "to be the best at everything", which even Gerhard Berger's daughter Christina noticed in Senna on their shared boat trips, is too deeply rooted. But even when he is dogged by bad luck in the grand finale while lying in second place and storming into the attack, and he is forced to retire with a mechanical defect, he is able to joke about it: "Better here than next year in the Williams..."

1994 should be his year. It *will* be his year – the experts agree on that. There can be only one aim: to be World Champion for the fourth time, and it seems to be within his grasp. Senna and Williams, the best driver in the best car – what could go wrong? And Ayrton himself is firmly convinced that this will be his great year, even if he always hedges his bets in public: "With the new rules, the ban on electronic aids, the cards are certain to be reshuffled," he declares in January at the official team presentation in Estoril. "Williams will certainly be more affected than others; everything will be much closer between the

A new car, a new season, and Senna watches the monitor showing the fastest lap times; at the start of the year he is everybody's clear favourite to become 1994 World Champion.

leaders. I don't see myself as the only favourite this year."

He keeps on making the observation that technically the cars will be much closer to each other. All the same, privately he adds with a slight smile: "But that doesn't necessarily have to be reflected in the results..."

One can feel that he is bursting with self-confidence. He seems to hold in his hands every opportunity to realize his dream, to show everybody once and for all how good he really is. He finds in this his new challenge and motivation, as much as in the new environment of working with a new team after six years with McLaren. Is he worried about the high expectations of him? "Not really, because I'm incredibly motivated, precisely by this change. I needed a new environment... And if I am motivated, then although people's expectations are certainly some pressure, I know that I can do it, that Williams and Renault will make their contribution. It's just a matter of finding the best way to co-operate. But then it should work out. As I said, this change was a very important step for me. The whole team is different, the people, the structures, a different engine manufacturer, different sponsors. Everything is new, everything different. And I must learn and adapt. Because I believe that's the right way: that I should adapt to the team and not expect that the team will adapt to me because I've been World Champion three times or whatever. I am one person, and there are 200 of them. So I must adapt, I must learn to understand their way of working, to adopt the good things from them – and perhaps with my experience at McLaren I can make a few suggestions about things that are not yet as good as they could be," he says in his typical way of expressing himself, threading ideas together, using repetition for emphasis, deliberately using the same words several times. That is his style – in any language: Portuguese, English or Italian.

How he gets the hang of the Williams so quickly, even with this positive attitude, is astonishing. By the first big test drive with the new car at the end of February it is quite clear: Williams is already a 'Senna team'. Damon Hill, who is after all an Englishman and with longer 'proprietorial rights', is soon playing a subordinate role. It is the accuracy of Senna's remarks that impresses the technicians, but also his motivation, his visible enthusiasm to throw himself into the work again. And also his way of treating people, of giving everybody, even the most junior of the mechanics, the feeling of recognition and importance.

Ayrton Senna feels quite at home in a go-kart, and at Bercy, in Paris, he enjoys himself immensely.

Senna is a master of doing this without it seeming artificial or manufactured. It comes from inside and it hits the mark. When in April, after the race at Aida, Senna comes of his own accord to the usual Williams post-Grand Prix Tuesday briefing at the works in Didcot, the staff are enthusiastic: "Nigel Mansell or Alain Prost never did that."

In Portugal in January he's still finding his feet, but he's sure in himself that he will find real friends at Williams, friends like Jo Ramirez, for example, the team co-ordinator at McLaren. "I've always found people like that in the teams I've been with before, with Toleman, Lotus and McLaren. So why not with Williams?"

Just to be sure, though, he takes one of his closest friends with him: Josef Leberer, his Austrian fitness coach, who has been looking after him since 1988 at McLaren, though his contract was always with the team. Josef has been pondering on what to do since October 1993. To go with Senna, who has asked him several times, or to stay at McLaren, where he feels really comfortable, where he is recognized and where they definitely want to keep him? It's a bit of a choice between heart and head, between feelings and commonsense, as he puts it himself on one occasion. Only in January, after Senna has phoned him a couple more times at home in Salzburg, does he decide in favour of the personal ties and goes with him – although officially again as team coach, responsible not only for Senna but also for Damon Hill. After Estoril he has pangs of conscience: "I haven't yet even spoken to Ron Dennis to tell him that I'm going."

Moving from McLaren to Williams is also a change of cigarette sponsor. When Senna sees Josef in Estoril sitting in the sun in

He rarely appeared as relaxed in public as he did at Bercy – he was full of hope for a fantastic year.

front of the Williams motorhome, a lighted cigarette in his hand, he promptly jokes: "Have you changed brands yet?"

The mood is relaxed this winter, at every test drive, at every appearance. With new motivation and new confidence, Ayrton seems younger than in 1992 and 1993. "Although I'm only 33 I've been in Formula 1 for 10 years now," he says, "and it does sometimes get a

bit tiring. Not physically, but psychologically, mentally. Through the constant pressure always to produce the best results, the expectation of having to win. That's exhausting. I believe that I am now at a stage where I had to change as much as possible in order to be motivated again and as a result to be successful. I think that from now on for me the key to success will be first and foremost to motivate myself properly. Because I know that I have the experience, the technical knowledge and also the talent in order to succeed. So motivation is decisive."

Decisive for attaining goals he has set for himself. That doesn't necessarily mean that he wants to beat Fangio's record of five World Championship titles or Prost's 51 Grand Prix victories. The figures come of their own accord, he believes: "Quite honestly," he admits, "the greatest number of Grand Prix victories is something that is not so far away, I think. The World Championship title is more difficult. A World Championship is always something bigger, over a longer period of time. I've won the title three times, so I know how difficult it is. Another two or even three is a lot of work – you can't plan for that. So my main aim is a bit different. My aim is to do everything as well as I can, as long as I am doing it. Then the victories, maybe even the World Championship, come on their own. Everything then automatically comes together."

So the priority is to keep up his motivation, to stay healthy and "clear in the head, in order to be able to achieve my full potential. Because I know I can do it, that I can win races, win a World Championship. I know it from the experience of having done it. I have a lot of experience on my side, that's a great help..."

"On the other hand," he muses, and this is one of the few occasions this winter when he allows himself a negative thought, "experience tells me that I shouldn't be too confident. I must be aware that I really have to give everything, use everything in order to be really good, really to achieve something. I mustn't allow myself to rely on the fact that I've done it before and that therefore everything will work

without problems. Because then things will definitely go wrong... It only needs a short moment, something that doesn't work properly – and everything can come to an end..."

But he doesn't want to dwell long on the shadows, and he adds at once: "All the signs are good. We just have to put it together properly."

How disappointed would he be if it didn't work, if at the end of the year he wasn't World Champion for the fourth time? The answer is a little sharper than usual – at least in tone: "I don't think so. I am convinced that one must think positively. One must move positively towards a goal, a task. As I have said, all the necessary factors seem to be there. Of course, motor racing is not predictable. A lot can happen. But one mustn't think negatively. Move forward positively, knowing that one can do it and then working to make it happen, that's my way."

His confidence and self-assurance are infectious. The inner peace which he has brought back from Brazil from his "winter summer holiday", during which he "worked a lot", promoted his businesses, "and finally got my helicopter licence, which I've wanted for ages", is fascinating. He is sitting in the house of his good friend Braga in Sintra, Portugal, only a few kilometres from the racetrack at Estoril, on the eve of the big Williams presentation, his first major appearance for his new team, and putting into words his wish for 1994:

"If at the end of this year I am still as happy as I am now, then it

A long day of practice at Imola comes to an end – but before he can have a well-earned rest he has to face the press.

At the 1994 Brazilian Grand Prix – together with Michael Schumacher: "We're competitors, not rivals!"

will have been a very good year, professionally and privately..."

In Le Castellet, at the end of February, he tests the new Williams FW16 thoroughly for the first time.

What Senna said...

January 1994

My aim is not to win a certain number of races this year, my aim is to give the maximum and to get the best out of myself.

My motivation is the search for perfection, the attempt to improve myself more and more, to go on learning. Perhaps one can never attain absolute perfection, but to get as close to it as possible, that is the aim.

If at the end of this year I am still as happy as I am now, then it will have been a very good year, professionally and privately.

It's a private Williams test, so there is no other team there and therefore no lap times for comparison. But the car seems to be OK.

Nevertheless, Senna is cautious: "We still have a lot to do. Besides, one never knows how things will go on other circuits."

But his manner shows that he is not really worried. Brazilian journalist Celso Itibeira of *O Globo* couldn't help noticing: "He has trouble suppressing a laugh when he speaks of problems."

Senna is uncomplicated, open, approachable: in the lunch break he joins the few journalists who are present at their table. No interview, just a relaxed chat. About his projects in Brazil, about his early days in Formula 1, his first practice here at Le Castellet 10 years ago with a Brabham-BMW: "When I arrived by train in Marseilles from

Milan and was standing there at the station, I didn't know how to get to my hotel or the track. Today my jet is standing by – not bad progress, is it?

Thierry Boutsen, one of Ayrton's best friends among his fellow drivers, drops by for a moment. He's brought his son Kevin with him, so Ayrton will have something to do in the break between practices – to play with Kevin. Because for Senna, children are the greatest thing. But there's no way the lad will allow the famous yellow helmet to be placed on his head, not even by the champion himself...

A week later, at Imola, comes the eagerly awaited comparison of the new Williams-Renault with the rest of the Formula 1 world: Senna

**Concentration – under the protection of ▷
the famous yellow helmet!**

Senna with his compatriot Christian Fittipaldi and Heinz-Harald Frentzen, with whom he gets on very well...

dominates the practice laps until the Friday evening, when suddenly Michael Schumacher, in flat-out qualifying style, conjures up a lap in 1 minute 21.0 seconds, just beating Senna's best time of 1:21.2.

Meanwhile, it is leaked that there was an internal Williams instruction not to drive with less than 60 litres of fuel in the tank; they didn't want to reveal their full potential.

Senna takes the 'defeat' very

Heinz-Harald Frentzen

Sauber-Mercedes team

Senna was a giant. For me he was always invulnerable... I had the good fortune to get to know him a bit better in the last few months. That we got on well meant a lot to me.

calmly: "The times here are not decisive. This is the end of the winter World Championship. The real thing will be seen in Interlagos." Confidence gleams in his eyes as he whispers to the Brazilian journalists: "Actually, I drove a quite different time to what is down on paper..." When one of them, astonished, asks how that could be, he grins: "By starting the lap somewhere else..." It's the old trick: somewhere out on the circuit you set your own start-and-finish point and time the lap there with your own internal timing equipment. Further inquiries with the team reveal it was probably a low 1:20 time – no wonder they were not particularly bothered by Schumacher's 1:21.0. "*Senninha* would probably have broken the record here," he comments, in an allusion to the comic-strip character

he has just created in Brazil, and that other 'Senninha', the younger Ayrton Senna, probably would have done so, too, in his wilder early years...

The Imola testing is over, and afterwards, even while he is talking to the press, he's on and off the phone to Frank Williams, a sentence here and a sentence there, but everything quite relaxed. Then he heads off to his car: "Ciao, my friends, I'm sorry, but I must be off."

Someone mutters after him: "Maybe you didn't set a new lap record, but there's definitely going to be a new record for the road to Bologna airport..." His plane is waiting there to take him to Paris. He wants to get the Varig flight to São Paulo the same evening so as to relax at home for a few days before facing the pressure of the home Grand Prix.

Interlagos will be the first real test, and it provides the first warning shot. Although he is quickest in every practice and qualifying period his advantage over Schumacher in the Benetton is less than generally expected. The Williams is not performing as well as it should. Ayrton blames the very uneven track: "I've said from the beginning that there could be problems with the car on very bumpy circuits. And I've also said that things will be closer..."

All the same – even if the official version is different – he hadn't really reckoned on such strong competition from Schumacher and Benetton. He acknowledges the young German driver's achievement: "Michael is a very good driver and he obviously has an optimal technical package behind him." But privately he's annoyed: "Always, when I think everything could go relatively smoothly for once, something or somebody gets in the way and makes it more difficult."

He takes the lead in the race, but loses it to Schumacher during the first routine pit-stops and is still behind him after they have both made their second stops. Towards the end he puts in a tremendous effort to close the gap, but he loses grip on a left-hand corner, slides to a halt and his engine stalls. His race is over, and so is the interest of tens of thousands of disappointed Brazilians, who make their way towards the exit long before the race ends.

But Senna is saddest of all: "For me it's the most disappointing when I can't give anything back to my fans here, who love me so much. It was obviously my mistake, but I needed to win here. A second place in Brazil would have meant nothing to me."

Before the Pacific Grand Prix in Aida, Japan, Williams tests the car once more in Jerez – they want to get on top of the problem with the aerodynamics, especially in slow bends, as manifested in Interlagos. But it turns out not to be so simple, whereupon Ayrton comes out with the comment: "Typical, I've hardly arrived at Williams and they promptly screw things up with the car" – in Portuguese a few nuances make the comment even stronger.

In Aida, again not the best track for the Williams, he once again wins pole position, but then has a bad start. And when he tries to get close in behind Schumacher "in order not to take any risks", Mika Häkkinen rams him from behind with his McLaren and he is out of the race almost before it has begun. Schumacher goes on to win again, so now he leads the World Championship duel 20:0 on points.

Senna tries to conjure up the confidence of the winter again: "There are another 14 races and I've been in more difficult positions in my career. Don't panic! We must just calmly keep on working and battle on."

But his eyes are no longer sparkling as they were a few weeks earlier. The winter, which was a summer, is getting colder again. The light at the end of the tunnel is what Senna would most like to see in Imola.

The first-corner crash at Aida: Mika Häkkinen has knocked Senna into a spin, and now Nicola Larini is about to hit the stranded Williams with his Ferrari.

"Winning is like a drug"

The finest triumphs of a dream career

There are some Formula 1 drivers who have already attained their goal when they simply take part in a race. For them, it doesn't matter if they are in last place on the starting grid and have no realistic chance of doing well – they are happy just to have made it into Formula 1. Others are not satisfied until they can at least race amongst the leaders, collect some points and perhaps occasionally earn a place on the winners' rostrum.

For Ayrton Senna there was always only one aim – to win. That others could think differently was quite alien to him: "I think to all of us, different feelings come and go, but one thing we all have in common, apart from all our differences – personality differences – is that we are all racers, we love our activity, we take chances, we take risks, we go through pain, we sacrifice a lot of things in life just for the pleasure to be number one."

◁ **The start in Adelaide in 1993 – it will be Senna's last duel with Prost and also, though nobody knew it at the time, Senna's last victory.**

A farewell present from Ron Dennis after six years with McLaren: a collage of the finest moments...

	World Champion	2nd	World Champion	World Champion	4th	
	1988	1989	1990	1991	1992	1993

"Winning is like a drug," he once said, during a run of great victories – and he admitted that he was almost addicted to this drug. He was able to experience its effect 41 times during his Formula 1 career, and fittingly, the last time – the Australian Grand Prix in 1993 – was for him one of his most important and finest victories.

Australia 1993 is a weekend of emotion: Senna's farewell from McLaren after six years and at the same time the last ever Grand Prix for his great rival Alain Prost. Senna, much more sensitive than many people realize, has a fine understanding of the mood. Parting is very difficult for him – even though he had wished for nothing with greater longing than finally to be able to drive a Williams. "But I'm leaving a lot of good friends behind. The whole time I've always

worked very well and very happily with everybody, with the mechanics and the engineers. It was a fantastic partnership, with all the successes, a unique time in my life. It's an era in my life which I am leaving behind."

On the starting grid the emotions break through. McLaren team co-ordinator Jo Ramirez, who in six years of working together with Senna has become a close friend, comes up to Ayrton's car and says: "If you win again here I'll love you for ever" – at which Senna can no longer hold back his tears. Five minutes before the start he's sitting in the car weeping without restraint.

"Jo is a good friend, he has a big heart and he is also very emotional. When he came to me I was also very moved. On the one hand it was a very beautiful experience, but

it was also dangerous because one should maintain full concentration. But it was also very beautiful, a test for me, to see with all my professionalism, with all the responsibility that I had, that the emotions which were within me could be expressed in a beautiful way at such a moment."

By the time of the start he has himself firmly under control again; he takes the lead straight away and seems to be completely in command all the way through the race. The Williams may still be the better car, but today Prost never really has a chance. Even so, McLaren chief Ron Dennis is pretty nervous in the McLaren pits, arguing first of all with Senna's race engineer Giorgio Ascanelli over the correct fuel consumption calculations and then with Senna himself over the radio about the right moment for the second pit-stop.

"How do you know about that?" asks Ayrton, completely taken aback when he's asked about the incident after the race. The answer is that French television had tuned in to the McLaren pit radio. "And I thought our radio was scrambled..."

Senna never seemed to be in any real danger of losing this Grand Prix. But, as he says afterwards, it was never easy: "It was a victory of strength of will, the will to do everything right from beginning to end, not to allow any mistakes, but also always to give the absolute maximum. For the whole race, in every lap, at every bend. That was the only way to win this race. With 90 per cent I wouldn't have won, I always had to give 100 per cent." That he succeeded in doing so gives him a special satisfaction: "It's not just winning that's special, but the way I did it. And that's something only I know exactly myself, because I experienced it, lived through it, felt it myself – at every bend, in every lap."

The finest moments come after the finish. As Senna climbs out of

Very good friends: Ayrton Senna and McLaren's team co-ordinator Jo Ramirez.

the car Ron Dennis takes him by the arm and whispers to the driver who has just given McLaren its 104th Grand Prix victory, thus making it the most successful team in the history of the World Championship: "It's never too late to change one's mind," says Dennis, perhaps hoping that he still might persuade him from going to Williams...

Then there is a short handshake with Alain Prost, and scenes of reconciliation on the victor's podium as Senna invites Prost, his `deadly enemy' for so long, and Damon Hill, his team-mate for next year, to join him on the top step of the podium.

"It was spontaneous, on the spur of the moment, it couldn't be otherwise, it couldn't end any other way. That's how it was, with us together on the podium after our race, a great moment for Formula 1, for the fans, with both of us at the end of an important era in our lives..." He won't say that everything that has happened has been forgiven. "But despite all the differences we are both sportsmen,

The invitation to the farewell party, which was arranged by the sponsor.

Reconciliation: Senna invites Alain Prost to join him on the victory podium in Australia, along with Damon Hill, his team-mate for 1994.

World Champions, we both love racing... One shouldn't say too much now, words here can only hurt and destroy... One should just leave things as they played themselves out. I believe it showed both my and his feelings. It was something that wasn't possible before – but at this moment it was possible." Adelaide 1993 is to be the last Senna victory, on November 7, 1993.

It's 29 years since his first step on the ladder, his first drive in a go-kart given to him by his father Milton, and 25 years since the first – unofficial – go-kart race which Senna contested as an eight-year-old against much older competitors. In those days places on the starting grid were chosen by lot, and Ayrton, being the youngest, draws the first lot and gets number one. "So in my first race I had pole position." For a long time he's in

the lead: "because I was small and light I could always pull away from the others on the straights." But shortly before the finish someone rams him from behind, and that's the end of beginner's luck. "But I still know that I enjoyed myself immensely."

He wins his first official race in Interlagos on July 1, 1973 – and then goes on year after year collecting every possible go-kart title in South America. What strikes one even then is his search for perfection in every area. Whether it's the technical preparation of the go-kart or his own desire to learn, he's not satisfied with half-measures. "The first time I drove a go-kart in the rain it was a disaster. I couldn't cope with it at all, everybody overtook me. So then, whenever it rained, I went to practise and in the course of time I got the hang of it..." Racing in the

rain is to become one of his greatest strengths...

In 1978 the conquest of the big world of international racing begins. Ayrton comes to Europe – at that time still under his own name, Ayrton da Silva. "But da Silvas are two a penny in Brazil." So, in order to stand out a bit, he soon adds his mother's maiden name and from then on the name Ayrton Senna da Silva appears in the lists of entries. And it stays that way until the early Eighties, when someone explains to him that it's too long and complicated – especially for the English journalists, who always have difficulties with foreign names anyway. So the 'da Silva' is finally removed and just Ayrton Senna remains. The pronunciation of his first name

Many more victories, many more great races, still seem to be in sight... ▷

causes enough problems, and for years all kinds of versions are heard in the racing world. His nickname `Beco' is simpler. He's had it since childhood, his sister Viviane having thought it up, but only family and close friends are allowed to use it...

There is one goal that he doesn't achieve in these first years in Europe: he never becomes go-kart World Champion, although he tries repeatedly with his already well-established and widely recognized determination, which at times can border on obstinacy. A couple of times he is close: at Estoril in 1979 and at Nivelles in Belgium in 1980 he comes in second. He is the fastest man in the field, but something always seems to go wrong. At one of these World Championship races, among the spectators there is an 11-year-old boy from Germany, who recalls: "I was so impressed by this guy in the yellow helmet that I looked in the programme to see who he was." The name of the young fan is Michael Schumacher...

Senna sits in a real racing car – a Formula Ford 1600 – for the first time in England in 1981. This is the last step away from Brazil towards a completely different and colder environment. At first he hardly understands the language, and he has to learn to adapt to a totally new lifestyle. Also, money is tighter than he is used to. His father's cheques don't flow so generously because at first he doesn't think much of his son's plans. Racing as a hobby was OK, but as a professional career, racing as a job? But Senna would not be Senna if these circumstances were to seriously deter him from his goal. And that means winning – winning at any cost, which is what he does: in the Formula Ford 1600 in 1981 he wins 12 out of 20 races, and in 1982 in the Formula Ford 2000 the score is 21 out of 27...

The race at the Jyllandsring, in Denmark, at which he finally secured the European Championship title in 1982 in the Formula Ford 2000, is an occasion he still remembers clearly 10 years later: "... especially because I had had so little sleep. The night before I'd found something much better to do than sleep... I still remember that she was very blond..." [By that time his marriage to his childhood friend Liliane had already ended.]

He was never the `victory machine' with no human features, no slip-ups, never looking to right or left, which was the way many people continued to describe him during his career. The aberrations were rare, perhaps, but there were some from time to time. For example, there was an occasion about a year later, by which time he had become British Formula 3 Champion after a fantastic struggle with Martin Brundle, which had gone to the very last race. With the first Formula 1 trials with Williams and McLaren behind him [they were part of his reward for becoming F3 Champion] he came for the first time to the famous Formula 3 classic in Macau. Although he didn't know the track, this didn't stop him from convincingly taking pole position, which seemed a good

At 18, poised to conquer Europe: at the go-kart World Championships in 1978 at Le Mans...

Always the fastest, but Senna never becomes go-kart World Champion...

Guerrero, the Colombian driver, who already had some Formula 1 experience, and Gerhard Berger, who soon realizes: "This is someone who's one level above the rest of us..."

In March 1984 Senna celebrates his Formula 1 debut in a Toleman at his home track in Brazil. A somewhat pale, slim young man, whose soft features nevertheless betray a lot of determination and seriousness. "For the first time I was really in the limelight with lots of people – journalists and fans – around me. Not a bad feeling then."

His race lasts for only eight laps, then he's forced out by engine failure. But only two weeks later in South Africa he comes in sixth, winning his first World Championship point. It is very hot, and as the chequered flag drops Senna is done for, totally exhausted, and has to be lifted from the car. "I was in such pain, as though millions of needles had bored into my body. I simply wasn't fit enough." His response is to take on his own fitness coach, Nuno Cobra, and get

enough reason to celebrate! "And so on Friday night, with a whole bunch of people, at least five or six, we set off... and got stuck in a bar with a few lemon vodkas."

For someone who usually hardly touches a drop of alcohol, a few lemon vodkas can be a disaster. "To this day I have no idea whether we even paid when we came out of this pub." And the next day – fortunately in Macau the Saturday is not a Formula 3 practice day – he is still in a complete daze. "I tried everything, I went running like a madman, but nothing helped. I couldn't clear my head, I still felt miserable."

On Sunday morning in the warm-up he drives two laps and then takes the car back to the pits, saying to his team: "Everything's fine, there's no need to do any more."

His mechanics look at him in astonishment – they've never come across this with Senna, the perfectionist. "But I was as shattered after those two laps as if I had driven two races one after the other, completely soaked in sweat, finished..." He drives back to the

hotel, stands under the shower and goes to bed for two hours – there's still time before the start.

"And when I woke up everything was OK. Apparently the tension of driving those two laps, the extreme strain and the sweating squeezed everything out." In the two-part race he wins both heats convincingly ahead of Roberto

The beginning of his career in England: Senna is almost unbeatable in Formula Ford races.

37

him to work out a personal training programme for him, which he then follows meticulously. Later, he pays regular visits to fitness expert Willi Dungl's clinic in Austria and works out there. The striving for perfection extends to his own fitness.

In Monaco, after only his sixth Grand Prix, Senna stands on the podium for the first time, having finished a close second behind Alain Prost and ahead of Stefan Bellof in a race which has been drowned by torrential rain and abandoned after 32 laps. With the rain having evened-out the performance of the cars, for once the drivers' skill has been allowed to play the decisive role, and the young Brazilian has stormed through from 14th place on the starting grid – a major step in establishing the legend of `Senna the rain king'. With Prost in trouble with his car and Senna closing fast, many experts are still convinced that race director Jacky Ickx deprived Senna of his first Grand Prix victory by calling off the race at the crucial moment.

"I would certainly have overtaken Prost, but what would have happened then one can't say," commented Senna later on one occasion; "perhaps I would have won, perhaps I would have

dropped out..."

It's raining again in Estoril in April 1985, but meanwhile Senna has changed teams: he's no longer in a Toleman, but in a black and gold Lotus. And for the first time in Formula 1 he's occupying the starting position which later will become virtually his own: right at the front – pole position. It's the second Grand Prix of the season, and Senna dominates it from the start in the style of a World Champion. He appears positively to glide through the rain, over the puddles on the track, seemingly oblivious to the dangers of aquaplaning. Where others go wrong and plough through the grass alongside the track or spin off, he takes the Lotus through the spray as though on rails and never seems to be in danger. At least, that is the outward appearance.

But later, he analyzed his own performance: "I was on the limit as well. There were quite a few moments when it was very tight, when I was afraid I would fly off." Nevertheless, at just 25 and in only his 16th Grand Prix, he seems to be

The world's attention is drawn to Senna's rising star by his brilliant performance in the rain at Monaco in 1984.

so incredibly in control that the first part of the legend is born here in Estoril – a name that will constantly accompany him in years to come: 'magic Senna'.

As he crosses the finishing line he raises both hands in the air in delight, and one of the first embraces as he climbs out of the car is from his mother Neide – and there are a few surreptitious tears. The joy on the victor's podium at Estoril is exuberant, but very soon he seems to have both feet firmly on the ground again with a very precise and clear analysis of racing. "The moments of joy in our sport are very intense but very short, and they have to be overlaid very quickly by normal work if you want to continue to be successful." He voiced this comment much later, long after he had made it abundantly clear how strongly this first victory had been etched in his memory, how important it had been to him. In answer to the question that was always asked of him about his 'finest moments', this race was always well to the fore.

If anything he seems to be embarrassed by the number of compliments which pour in from around the world after this triumph in Estoril. Shyness overcomes pride, at least on the outside. It is this shyness which in the early years often prevents him from looking someone straight in the eye, which makes him answer critical or awkward questions with a brusque-sounding "I don't care", which is very soon interpreted as arrogance. In reality, behind it lies first and foremost an attempt to protect a very sensitive inner core, to protect it from the hardness and coldness with which he is confronted in Formula 1. "After all, I came from a relatively sheltered world, from the warmth of my family."

As time passes, he withdraws more and more into himself,

especially after he feels that he has been badly disappointed and deceived by the media. This feeling is heightened by the affair during the winter of 1985-86, when he refuses to accept Derek Warwick as his Lotus team-mate and is crucified by the British press in particular; the episode leaves its mark. "I've always tried to explain that it was nothing to do with Derek personally, nor with my not wanting to have strong competition within the team." The reason was that he was convinced – probably with some justification – that Lotus

team-mate who also has pretensions to be number one."

At the time he is deeply hurt that he is universally reproached for cowardice on the one hand and for inappropriate interference in team decisions on the other. His relationship with a part of the British press never returns to normal after this, and the rest of the press has to wait a long time before being permitted to see some of Senna's more attractive personal features which have been hidden behind the facade of a cool man dedicated to and consumed by success, striving only for victories and the World Championship title. There is no question that on the race track Senna works more intensely, with a higher level of concentration and commitment, than anybody else, that during the race weekend he subordinates everything to one aim – to win. But there is much more to him than this...

The mask cracks for the first time in 1988 at Suzuka, in Japan, when the emotion at finally achieving his great goal, his first World Championship title, sweeps everything else away.

The situation at Suzuka is clear: it is the penultimate race of a year in which McLaren-Honda has convincingly dominated the competition. Senna, the new boy on the team, who arrived from Lotus at the end of 1987, has shown himself to be unmistakably faster than twice World Champion Alain Prost, who has been with McLaren since 1984 and around whom the team's recent successes have largely been moulded. In terms of practice lap times he has been beaten by Prost only twice in the whole season. Usually, he is also

would not be in a position to prepare two cars to an equally high standard, and he was afraid that there would be major internal struggles for resources and supremacy if there was a strong English driver in the team. "There were the first signs of something like that happening in 1985 with Elio de Angelis and me. I was convinced that if I was to have a chance of competing for the World Championship with Lotus then the major team effort had to be concentrated on one car. And that doesn't work when you have a

The combination of man and machine is ▷
the key to success in Formula 1. The
Renault engine takes Senna to his first
four victories.

What Senna said...

1984

I know what I can expect from myself
and my team. I am not a gambler. I do
things in a programmed way.

I would like to be respected for what I
do.

Self-confidence is the elixir of life for
the racing driver. Whoever doesn't
believe himself to be very, very good
had better give up.

1985

My ideal was to be able to combine
the qualities of Fittipaldi, Piquet, Lauda
and Stewart.

You can learn something from
everybody. I always keep my eyes
open, it would be stupid to think you
can already do everything.

I know myself – I am generally very
direct. Because I'm like that some
people think I'm puffed up and
arrogant. Sometimes that bothers me
a bit, because I'm sure that I'm not.

Racing is everything for me, it is the
challenge of my life, it is a profession
and a vocation, a hobby and at the
same time a virus which has no cure. I
have lost interest in everything else,
my soul and my body belong to racing.

1986

I perceive my successes and my
achievements as quite normal. I have
been racing as long as I can
remember. I had the opportunity to
learn this sport from the bottom up. I
also give my best, so I see success as a
quite normal development.

I would like to push myself to the limit
in everything I do.

What does it matter to me what other
people say or write? I try to give my
best, that's all.

1987

Formula 1 is big business and a big
responsibility – that takes away some
of the fun.

I have complete respect for Prost, not
only as a driver, for his racing, but also
for the way in which he gives himself
and what he has achieved.

rooted to the spot: the engine has
died on him. He already has his
arms up to warn the drivers behind
him, and his first piece of luck is
that nobody drives into him. The
second is that the starting and
finishing straight at Suzuka is on a
downward slope. "I'd thought that
all was lost, but I let the car roll
forward and it seemed to pick up,
then the engine gave out again. So
I did the same, and this time I finally
got going, slowly at first, but going
all the same. It was real luck..."

He gets away from the starting
line in 14th place and Prost is in the
lead. At the end of the first lap he is
eighth. But chasing Prost seems a
hopeless task because the leader
has the advantage of a clear track
ahead of him, so can usually lap
faster and extend his advantage.
But Senna tries everything. His lack
of compromise, usually to be seen
most impressively when passing
other drivers, stands him in good
stead. On the second lap he
overtakes Riccardo Patrese and
Alessandro Nannini to take sixth
place. He is now 9 seconds behind
Prost. On the third lap he beats his
friend Thierry Boutsen and moves
up to fifth, but he's lost another
second on Prost. Overtaking costs
time... On the fourth lap it's
Alboreto's turn: now he's in fourth
place, but 12.9 seconds behind,

faster in the races – but the
occasional mistake and a few
strange technical problems,
especially in the two races
preceding Suzuka, have left Prost
still in the running for the title. The
Frenchman comes to Japan with six
wins, Senna with seven. Only at
Monza has there been a win for
other than a McLaren driver – and
Gerhard Berger only won for Ferrari
on that occasion because, two laps
from the finish and with the race
seemingly won, Senna collided with
the Williams of the inexperienced
Jean-Louis Schlesser. But a victory in
Japan can conclusively put Senna's
first world title in the bag. However,
if Prost wins, the decisive race will

have to be the last one in Adelaide.
That Ayrton once again secures
pole position – for the 12th time in
the year – is hardly a surprise. But
the fact that he totally mucks up
the start – "definitely the most
important of the year" – certainly is.
As the light turns green he stays

Martin Brundle

**McLaren-Peugeot,
and former
Formula 3 rival**

I can't say that I knew
Senna particularly well on
the human level, but I did

professionally. We fought
hard against one
another, but always
within the bounds of
what is permitted. What
immediately impressed
me about him were his
professionalism and his
dedication. It was clear

from the first moment,
from the first race, that he
was something special. He
always seemed to know
instinctively where the
limit was. Not after the
bend, but before it. As
though he could see every
reaction in advance...

and a lap later the gap is over 13 seconds. "But then I gradually got into a rhythm and got faster and faster."

Up to lap 10 he nibbles away at Prost's lead a few tenths of a second at a time. He's 11.6 seconds behind when he catches up with Gerhard Berger and takes third place from him, then he makes up more ground. Ahead, Prost is surprised to see young Ivan Capelli in the March in his rear-view mirror – and a look at the sky bodes no good for him, either: there are dark clouds threatening rain, and Senna's ability in the wet is all too well-known. On lap 14 the first drops of rain fall. It's not really wet, but the track becomes a bit slippery. On lap 16 Capelli actually passes Prost to hold the lead for a short time, but the Frenchman is able to counterattack. Senna, meanwhile, is getting ever closer, catching up by as much as 2 seconds a lap, and on lap 20 he gains almost 5 seconds. "Because I had problems with my gearbox," says Prost later.

Senna has barely caught up with the two leaders when Capelli drops out with engine trouble. The two challengers for the world title are now alone in a straight duel – symbolic of the whole season, if not of a whole era.

It lasts until lap 27, then Senna goes past at the end of the start-finish straight. The battle is over. Prost is unable to counterattack, even though temporarily it stops raining. "I kept on having problems with the gears – and I lost a lot of time in the traffic..." It's the old story: Senna overtakes traffic harder and tighter than anybody else. He

Ayrton can finally celebrate his title – with Honda chief Soichiro Honda.

builds up his lead. Two laps from the end it's grown to 9 seconds. Then the rain returns, if anything heavier than before. A few times Senna points to the sky, demanding that the race be ended, but the officials don't react. "It's raining much harder behind me, at the other end of the track." So he has to wait, he has to live with the tension all the way to the 51st and last lap, to the last bend. As he turns into the finishing straight he takes one hand from the steering wheel and raises a clenched fist; he knows his dreams are about to be fulfilled. As he crosses the line he throws both hands into the air in celebration, again and again, almost all the way down to the first bend. He has his race engineer Steve Nichols on the radio, and he positively shouts over and over again into his ear: "We've done it, we've done it." And then he allows

himself to slump back for a moment, resting his head briefly against the back of the cockpit. The tension of a whole year, perhaps even of several years, gives way and dissolves into tears. At the television press conference his eyes are still red from them and he is overcome by emotion: "I still can't believe that it's over. The season was so long, for Alain and for me, it was an unbelievably hard struggle, and although we always tried to make it less painful for each other the pressure was dreadful," he said, his voice still almost choking on the barely suppressed emotion.

The tears keep on coming, even late in the afternoon when he's once more in the pits, giving television interviews. The film of the race is being shown again on the huge video wall display. "You were so focussed on your goal that you sacrificed many friendships on the

◁ **The first world title – after a hard struggle against Alain Prost the dream finally comes true in Suzuka: "But the pressure was dreadful."**

way up, you shoved people aside. Now that the pressure is off, will it be different?" he's asked by Reginaldo Leme of Brazilian television. The answer is fresh tears running down his face. In the evening he enjoys his greatest triumph to date – which will remain to the end "the finest moment of my career" – in a very special way. Fuji-TV has given him a video recording of the race, without commentary, but with the original soundtrack, and has also fixed up a video recorder in his room in the Suzuka Circuit Hotel. Quite alone, in the darkness in front of the television, he relives in thought and picture "the best race in my life so far".

Over the next two years, which are dominated by his battle with Alain Prost, he wins 12 more races, and in 1990 comes his second World Championship, by which time he has become a different person. He opens up more, something that could be detected from the end of 1989, after the low of losing the world title to Prost in Suzuka, with all the ugly circumstances which surrounded it. "I've made some mistakes myself in dealing with the media," he admits, and then he begs: "Let's make a fresh start..." Now one can see his

other side again. But many people don't want to any more.

The old image remains. The change means fewer swings of mood, more peace — apart from a few exceptions. What remains is the commitment and the uncompromising will to win. "I drive only to win. Nothing else satisfies me," he keeps on saying. The emotion which he seeks in Formula 1 he finds in getting closer to perfection.

Especially in Brazil. Nowhere else was a victory so important for him. In 1991 it is the eighth attempt to win his home Grand Prix, so that at last he could give back to his public, which always acclaims him for the entire weekend, "all the joy, these feelings that people express to me".

1991 looks like giving him his best ever chance. It's the second race of the season, and Senna is coming to Interlagos from a

The start of the finest, but also the hardest race in Senna's career: Interlagos 1991, his first win at home.

convincing victory in the opening Grand Prix in Phoenix, Arizona. Interlagos, a southern suburb of his home city of São Paulo; Interlagos, where his career began in a go-kart, where he knows every centimetre, where a section of the circuit is

47

named after him... It's the Grand Prix that on the one hand he looks forward to more than any other, but which also brings him more strain than any other. First of all because of the high expectations – not only that others have of him, but also that he has of himself. And secondly because the melee is a bit bigger here than elsewhere. The 50 metres on foot from the helicopter to the pits can become a problem here, a battle not to be crushed by euphoric fans or battered or stabbed by countless curious reporters with cameras and microphones. This is particularly difficult for him. For if there is one thing he hates it is not having a little space in which to breathe and to move. When people press too close to him, when he is constantly being touched, he finds it extremely unpleasant, whether it is in the crush of fans, or of journalists. "Give me a little space" – how often has he voiced this almost desperate plea?

Yet in Brazil he copes remarkably well with it – probably because he feels and appreciates the love and the respect behind the tumult. When he comes to the circuit on the Thursday he has his first cause to celebrate: it's his 31st birthday. The cream-cake fight in the otherwise clinically clean McLaren pit is wild, with several mechanics and even photographers taking part. In the end Senna has a large part of the cake on his face. He manages to take it with good humour. But then he gets cross when he discovers that someone has nicked an envelope with tickets for his friends and guests which he had put down with his famous blue Nacional cap. Furious, he stomps through the pit, now littered with bits of cream cake, kicking the odd box – and precisely at that moment Ron Dennis comes through the door. The always correct,

meticulous and orderly head of McLaren clasps his hands to his head in horror. But he brings some order back to the team – and on Saturday Senna gets his pole position according to plan, although only with a powerful last-minute show of strength in order to squeeze out Riccardo Patrese, who is already giving a hint of the strong competition there will be from Williams this year. He put in a time of 1:16.775, and as the clocks stop at 1:16.392 for Senna's last lap before the chequered flag a roar and a wave of enthusiasm sweeps through Interlagos, as though Brazil had just won the football World Cup in the Maracana stadium.

It's the first step towards a home triumph – but nobody dreams of the drama that the Sunday of the race will bring. It's going to be a race that will go down in history, full of emotion, full of changing fortunes, full of class, and full of struggle and commitment to the absolute limit – a real Senna race.

The start is actually quite normal. Ayrton wins the sprint away from the line and is in the lead from the beginning, but he can't get away from Nigel Mansell, who's always within striking distance, putting on the pressure. Senna knew very well from the first practice session the previous day that "we won't necessarily have the fastest car here, that it will be very difficult against the Williams". And in this early stage of the race he has to drive much faster than he really wants in order to stay in front, "in order to have at least a few seconds in hand, for example in order not to get into critical situations when overtaking".

A familiar scene: surrounded by journalists, but Senna hates like the plague being hemmed in by a crowd, although rarely can he do anything about it...

Until he drops out, Nigel Mansell in the Williams-Renault proves to be a tough opponent for Senna in 1991 in Brazil.

Senna's tyre change couldn't go better, but he still can't feel secure. Only when Mansell has to make a second pit-stop on the 50th lap because he has damaged a tyre does he feel a certain relief. But only for a short time, because then he begins to have problems with his own car: "First of all fourth gear wouldn't engage, I had to change straight from third to fifth. Then other gears started to fail and jumped out. The gearbox was really playing up. It was extraordinarily demanding to drive like that. With my right hand I had to hold onto the gear stick, which was a bit loose, and steer only with the left hand, and make sure I didn't get into the wrong gear."

Is his home victory going to elude him yet again? Mansell is getting closer again – but on the 60th lap the Brazilian fans rejoice when the Englishman spins at the end of the start-finish straight – he has gearbox problems, too. As he tries to drive on "there are no gears there". Rumour has it afterwards that he spun the car with such force that the driveshaft broke.

Once again Senna has a bit of breathing space. After all, now he has a good 40-second lead over Riccardo Patrese. But suddenly his lap times become dramatically slower; he's losing 6 or 7 seconds per lap to the Italian. "Seven laps before the end I couldn't get into any gear at all." He is in despair, as he recalls afterwards: "I'm going to lose this victory after all," I tell myself, "after I've fought so hard. My shoulders, my arms, everything was hurting terribly." In a state of panic, and with a last spark of hope from which he draws strength once more, he tries again – and actually manages to get into a gear. It's sixth, the only one that still works,

and he stays in it till he reaches the finishing flag, not daring to risk changing a gear any more. "But it's incredibly difficult to drive so long in sixth gear. When you have to brake from 300km/h to 70 without being able to change down, the engine is still pushing you forwards on full power. I was very often on the brink of sliding off!"

He tries to adapt to the changed situation: "You can't take the slow bends so slowly. If the revs drop too much you have the danger of stalling. I had to change my driving style completely." He manages to do this so skilfully that soon he's losing only 2 or 3 seconds per lap. In the McLaren pit they've been biting their nails for a long time. While all the commentators in the television box are puzzled, in the pit they know all about the problem. Riccardo Patrese, who is still making up ground, also knows that Senna has problems. But he is torn. What should he do? Risk a final attack? But his car isn't running at its best, either, the Williams automatic gearbox sometimes taking on a life of its own. Should he fight for victory and risk an accident? Or play safe for second place? Riccardo is inclined to the second option, especially during the last two or three laps when it begins to rain, at first softly, then harder and harder.

But Senna knows nothing of Patrese's dilemma. He can only look in his mirror: "Where is he, how big is the gap, can I see him yet? How many more laps?" This time, even the rain is no help to him: "I know this circuit well, I knew exactly which direction the rain was coming from, which spots would get wet first. But with such a dodgy car it now became even more difficult to keep control. On the slow bends I had to drive even more slowly."

He can hardly believe that Patrese hasn't quite caught up yet, and he gathers himself for a final supreme effort in the cockpit: "I've always said to myself it's OK, you can do it, it'll work..." And he prays, as he later admits, "that I can get through, that the car will last out to the flag, that I might keep this victory. I believe that God gave me this victory."

The McLaren has scarcely crossed the finishing line when the engine finally dies and the car rolls to a halt. Senna tries to relax for a few moments, but he can't. At the instant he lets go and allows his absolute concentration to lapse "the pain hits me. In my arms and my shoulders, incredibly intense, incredibly strong." For several minutes he sits motionless in the car. "I didn't know whether I should scream, cry or laugh, I could hardly move. But I definitely wanted

to go onto the podium here for the award ceremony. Finally, Wilson Fittipaldi helped me to get out..."

A race-track management car brings him back to the pits. As he gets out, even before he climbs laboriously onto the victors' podium, fighting back tears of joy and pain, one of the first people to congratulate him is his father. He embraces him; it's only a short moment, but one filled with immense feeling. As he finally stands on the podium, the Brazilian flag in his right hand and the cup in his left, his strength leaves him. He wants to hold the cup up high, but he can't quite manage it and Ron Dennis has to help him. "For the moment I can't think at all or say anything, my head's empty. I am only immensely happy." These are his first words before he's able to say anything about this dream – and nightmare – race.

Too exhausted to lift the trophy after his hardest victory, Ron Dennis offers a hand.

Then, as soon as possible, he wants to be with "the team, my friends, my family". He is still walking stiffly, he can't move properly. Josef Leberer massages him for over an hour in the McLaren pit: "Everything was so tense, I've never experienced anything like it. It will probably last for days until it's gone completely. What he must have put into those last laps is almost superhuman." But a good two hours after the end of the race he's already feeling better. A crowd of Brazilian fans who have waited in front of the McLaren pits cheer him.

He thanks them, visibly touched, and the few people who have come back into the pits to congratulate him even get an embrace. The fact that he has stopped distancing himself is proof of his exuberance.

He can taste the joy of winning at home just one more time, in 1993; on the one hand it is 'only' a repeat, on the other it is incredibly fine, "quite different from '91, because it was totally unexpected". This victory is won with inferior equipment, through the best use of favourable circumstances. The rain, and Prost's mistake in delaying much too long his tyre change and skidding off the track. This time he can enjoy the success even more because he is fit. When he climbs out of the car he can be acclaimed by his public. And he celebrates until five in the morning at a huge party in the posh Limelight Disco in São Paulo, exuberant, carefree, "over the moon", as he puts it himself. He feels the after-effects "for almost a week, it was the wildest celebration I can remember". And this is the night when he meets Adriane, a 19-year

This time Senna can enjoy the euphoria of the fans: victory in Interlagos in 1993.

old photographic model, Adriane Galisteu, who is soon seen ever more often at his side, even at the racetrack, which is something very much out of the ordinary for him...

But Adriane was not with Ayrton for the European Grand Prix at Donington, two weeks after Brazil, so she missed perhaps the greatest triumph of his whole career. Even the first lap taken in isolation will go down in motor racing history as an epic performance.

The track is wet, but shortly before the start the rain has almost stopped. Nevertheless, nearly everybody – including Senna – will be starting on wet-weather tyres. Ayrton doesn't even manage a good start, and from fourth on the grid he immediately slips down to fifth. But after a short but hard duel with Michael Schumacher he's soon back up to fourth place. Then he moves swiftly up to third by going past Karl Wendlinger, who has managed an excellent start, on the outside. Damon Hill is his next target and he quickly disposes of him halfway round the lap. He then closes on Alain Prost, in the lead, cuts inside him at the hairpin, and the Frenchman can do nothing about it. Senna completes his stupendous first lap clearly in the lead, and by the end of the second lap he has opened-up a gap of about 6 seconds.

Throughout the race, conditions are changing constantly. The track dries out, then it rains again, sometimes harder, sometimes more softly. It's becoming a tactical race, with much depending on the precise timing of tyre changes – but most of all on a driver's delicate feel of the track and his judgment of his

Unbounded joy after his second home victory: and five-times World Champion Juan-Manuel Fangio, whom Senna admires greatly, congratulates him warmly.

What Senna said...

1988

The mistake in Monaco [where he crashed late in the race while holding a comfortable lead] was a turning point for me in this season. I and my family were strengthened by it, I got a lot of spiritual strength from it. It was only this mistake which finally gave me the strength to withstand the pressure of this season.

Yes, I cried as I drove through the finish. I couldn't believe it, I just couldn't believe that it was over. [In Suzuka.]

My only motivation in Formula 1 is to be successful. If I was just driving along with everybody else, then I couldn't justify my job as a racing driver to myself.

1989

Racing is in my blood and the present situation merely motivates me to fight against it. I have thought of giving up, but I am a professional, I have responsibility. And I am also a human being. The values that I have in my life are stronger than the desire of other people to influence or destroy these values. I refuse to run away from a fight. That is my mentality. [In Adelaide.]

Perhaps I have made mistakes,

especially in dealing with the media. I have generalized too much from isolated bad experiences. I must try to make a new start. [Also in Adelaide.]

1990

I have long since lost my respect for Prost.

Religion, faith in God, is important for inner balance which helps you to solve problems. When I am in a state of complete peace and inner security I can give my best to my work. Praying helps me to find confidence in myself and my abilities – but I don't pray to win.

Life is something that God gives us. In many instances it is up to us to show God that we understand that we regard health and life as a very great gift. It is our responsibility to look after such a gift.

1991

We are simply totally different, I have my upbringing and he has his. I go my way, and he goes his. I can only say that I am happy on my way, whether he is on his, I don't know. [About Prost.]

My aim is to win by always giving my absolute best and coming as close as possible to absolute perfection.

I am at the moment dependant on winning. The satisfaction, the feelings, that I get from winning, is what drives me on.

car's absolute limit of adhesion, plus his ability to adapt himself instantly and consistently to the ever-changing conditions.

And in such extreme circumstances, Senna outclasses everybody, in particular Prost, whose car is recognized as the best. Senna changes his tyres four times, Prost seven times. Ron Dennis would speak afterwards of a great team success, but in the main it is

Senna himself who decides when or even whether he is going to make a pit-stop. Sometimes, when the track is damp, he is lapping 3 seconds faster on dry tyres than Prost can manage on his wet tyres, and at one stage he has lapped the entire field. Only towards the end, when Senna's victory is assured, does Damon Hill, who by now has taken second place from Prost, manage to re-pass Senna in order

to be less than a lap behind at the finish.

Senna's victory gives him great satisfaction, and so it should because he has earned it by both out-driving and out-thinking the opposition. On the victor's podium he seems to be on cloud nine, and afterwards he is the undisputed sovereign. When Prost begins to list all the problems he had with his car, Senna just grins at him:

"Perhaps we should change cars," he suggests, a remark that does the Frenchman's self-confidence no favours whatsoever. No matter what comes next – after all Senna is still in the middle of delicate negotiations with McLaren for the 1993 season, and consequently only driving for them on a race-to-race basis – Ayrton has to admit: "It was worth coming back this year, just for this day".

Niki Lauda phones his congratulations: "I've never seen a race like it. You did the best that was humanly possible, the best that could possibly be done under those conditions. This was your best race yet!"

And Senna himself knows what a masterpiece it was. "A statement of an art," he calls Donington. And he adds: "This race left no room for dialogue, it was a monologue."

The legendary first lap at Donington in 1993: first of all there is a brief fight with Schumacher...

Nevertheless, he sticks to his philosophy: "There must always be room for improvement, I still want to believe that the next race can be even better. My best race – I'm always expecting it will be one that I drive in the future. I need that, it's a part of my motivation."

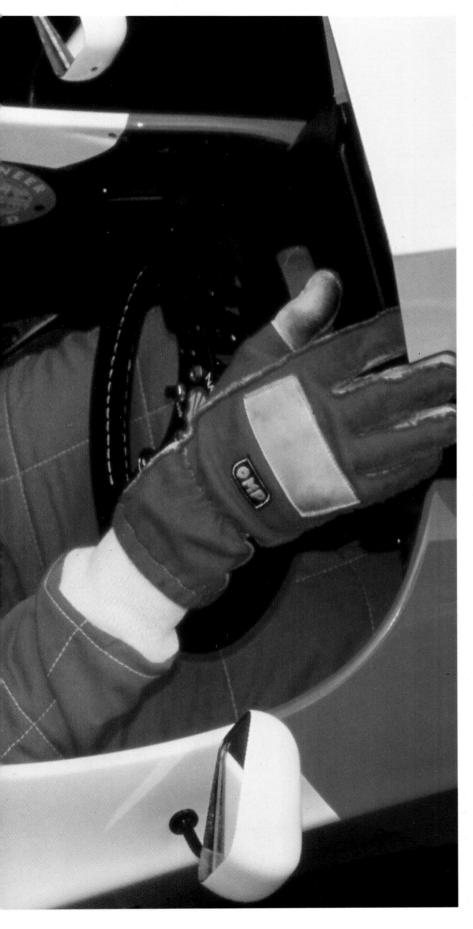

"I must learn to have patience"

The difficulty of dealing with failure

If you look only at the triumphs, 1993 was a great year for Ayrton Senna. But that is only half the truth. For a habitual winner like Senna, in reality 1993 was in many ways a very hard test, just as the year before had been...

After the third world title in 1991, 1992 was to bring the frustration of a technical collapse. Senna is forced to admit that under normal circumstances he can achieve nothing in the McLaren-Honda against the Williams-Renaults, nor can he see any great prospects for the future. From the middle of the year it becomes clear that McLaren will lose the Honda engines, and however much Ron Dennis fights to secure Renault engines the chances never look particularly good. For Senna this puts a huge question mark over McLaren for 1993, so where next? At Ferrari they can promise him only lots of hard work, but no winning car. So only Williams remains, and Senna definitely wants to go to them. He reckons that only they can offer him any real chance of success

Before every success there has to be perfect preparation – every detail must be right.

for 1993, and he has no desire whatsoever to be just driving along behind everybody else: "I'd rather have a year off, like Prost this year," he announces for the first time in the summer, at Silverstone.

The threat, however, is an empty one – it's an attempt to avert a development which is actually already under way. Alain Prost, Senna's great rival for the past five years, took up the option of a contract with Williams for the 1993 season very soon after he was sacked by Ferrari at the end of 1991. By spring 1992 the deal is virtually signed and sealed and includes a clause which is very important to Prost: Senna must not be his team-mate – at least for the first year.

"Because it would never work, as we know from the past," Prost says privately. "Because he's afraid of real competition, because he's a coward," Senna responds furiously, when he learns in Portugal in September that all his attempts to join Williams have failed. He even offered to drive for nothing, "in order to show how strongly I want to get this car..."

Frank Williams has been dreaming for ages of the 'dream-team' of Senna and Prost, but Alain refuses to be persuaded and insists on his clause, which says in effect: "If you get Senna, then I go." It is probably Renault who make the final decision between the two superstars. When all's said and done, they would very much like to have a French World Champion.

Senna, badly disappointed, once again becomes very emotional and can hardly come to terms with this defeat at a level of politics which he considers typical of Prost. He also reacts with a degree of defiance: "Perhaps I should consider pressing on at any price, just so as not to give him a clear run without a fight."

But his mood swings. Should he give up, and so avoid having to go through another year in which the frustration of having no chance of winning outweighs the fascination of driving? But should he give up – and thereby let Prost have the world title without a fight? Or should he take up the challenge after all, and look for a chance where nobody else sees one? Should he take the risk of having to give still more than he is already giving, perhaps venturing to the extreme limits of danger? Or should he think of alternatives which hitherto have seemed remote: America and the Indy Car series, for example?

During the two weeks between the last two races of the 1992 season, in Japan and Australia, Senna is very pensive, undecided and a little bit unsure of himself. He really seems not to know what he should do. Deep down he really wants to drive. Sometimes he looks almost desperately for explanations to justify carrying on with McLaren. This despite his earlier statements, for example in Spa, where he said that he is 99 per cent certain that he will leave McLaren and have a year off.

Of course, the Prost challenge is one factor, but he finds other reasons: "There are hardly any drivers of my generation... On the one hand there are those who are considerably older, and then the very young ones – but who is there

of us? Apart from Gerhard and Martin Brundle there aren't many..." And he reflects on his responsibility to the public and to his fans: "I can give a lot to them, I know it..." If one has to change one's life, one's direction for good reasons, then that's alright. "But when it happens for the wrong reasons, then it's bad, and I feel bad about it..."

But he also leaves the door open in case he withdraws: "We can't know why many things happen the way they do. Perhaps for some reason I simply shouldn't drive next year, it's predestined. Such things are not always necessarily in our hands..."

Many of those who know him

Very little of the glamour of Formula 1 remains on the lonely test drives – only hard work.

best believe that to take a year off, as Prost did in 1992, and then come back, is impossible for him. If he goes, then he goes for good because in that time he would find something else to do that would give him 100 per cent fulfilment. "I don't know," he says after long reflection, "I really don't know, everything is possible..."

On the other hand would he last out without racing at all? He, of all people, who believes that racing in a way is like a drug, "something on which one becomes dependant – and it's been proved that the human body in certain stress situations produces drug-like substances such as adrenalin..." Here too the same uncertainty and the unspoken plea: "Please don't press me. I really don't know the answers myself."

He comes to Adelaide, the last race of the season, which is also the farewell race of Nigel Mansell, the new World Champion, who is leaving for the American Indy Car series. The two of them fight bitterly for the lead once again, until their last appearance together ends with a collision. "Because Mansell braked 50 metres too early and caught me by surprise. I was so close behind him that I couldn't help driving into him," says Senna, who after dropping out watches the remainder of the race on the screen in the McLaren pits, keeping his fingers crossed for his team-mate Gerhard Berger. He is trembling with excitement, and at the end he is delighted at Gerhard's victory. Mansell, of course, sees things differently, saying that the collision was "deliberate". He runs to the sport's authorities to protest, but doesn't even get any support from his own team. Today's precise

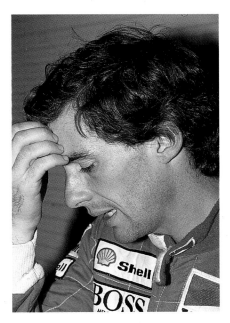

The frustration of two years without top material...

telemetry data show exactly where a driver brakes... That Mansell rushed away from the track, furious, after the crash and that there was no "goodbye" between the two long-standing adversaries is a bit disppointing for Senna: "I would have liked to have said farewell to him with a handshake after so many years together in Formula 1."

When he leaves himself, saying goodbye as usual to all his mechanics and technicians, acting quite normally and without showing any particular emotion, one can't help feeling that he doesn't really believe that he won't be coming back.

He does skip the grand McLaren end-of-season party at the Adelaide Hilton on the Sunday night, but that evening he comes to an agreement with Ron Dennis: "You see what kind of engines you can get, and when the new car is ready in January or February I'll give it a test and decide then."

But at this stage nobody says anything in public, so speculation continues to be rife. The Italians continue to link his name with

Ferrari, although Gerhard Berger and Jean Alesi already have contracts with them, not that this necessarily means much in Formula 1... And Senna plays along with them, letting slip a throwaway remark: "Everybody knows that I've always wanted to drive a Ferrari," and the comment "anything can happen..." It can't be so bad, perhaps, if Ron Dennis is made to believe that his superstar has other options.

At the beginning of December McLaren officially announces what everybody has already guessed: in 1993 they will drive with Ford engines, but as a client team, which means that contractually they will be in a weaker position than Ford's partners Benetton. Shortly before Christmas Senna tests a Penske Indy Car in Phoenix, Arizona – his friend Emerson Fittipaldi, a regular Penske driver, has arranged it. And he expresses enthusiasm: "At last, real driving again, not so much technology; as a driver one can still really do something."

These are sentiments that must give a shock to the Formula 1 authorities. If they lose Senna as well as Mansell to America, Formula 1 will have enormous problems. Ayrton knows that very well and does nothing to end the speculation, "although America was never really on the cards", as his cousin and manager Fabio Machado is to say later. At the end of January the game of poker with Ron Dennis begins, even before Senna comes to Europe for the first test. He considers the first financial proposals to be totally unacceptable. Dennis, who knows him very well from five years together, makes an initial offer of only $5 million. Senna wants $15 million,

Senna has to live with dropping out a lot in 1992, and dropping out in Japan is especially hard to take – his last race with a Honda engine on home ground.

which is a concession compared with the previous year. In this game, both of them have their trump cards. Dennis knows that Senna definitely wants to drive – and that he has no alternatives. And Senna knows that Dennis urgently needs him: only with Senna does McLaren have at least a small chance of posing a threat to Williams in the World Championship. Besides, their large tobacco sponsor Marlboro is pressing in the background for a superstar in the team.

On February 10, at the FISA meeting in Paris, McLaren suddenly name Michael Andretti and Mika Häkkinen as their drivers for 1993. Ron Dennis obviously wants to put on a bit of psychological pressure, and it seems to work; after a lot of excitement in the Senna office in São Paulo – where Fabio Machado is taken totally by surprise by the news – and a few long telephone conversations between England and Brazil, where Senna is enjoying the sun at his house by the beach in Angra dos Reis, there is a supplementary announcement the next day from the team nominating the triple World Champion as well. Under the new rules a team can name three drivers for two places...

At the end of February Senna duly tests the McLaren-Ford, "even though the other problems have only partially been solved". But time is pressing: there are only two weeks to the opening race of the season in South Africa. He is, as he says, "positively surprised" at how well the car goes, and at first sight he finds it extremely fast as well. He drives in the South African Grand Prix at Kyalami and takes second place, but still there is no contract, only an agreement from race to race.

The game between Senna and Dennis over the ensuing months becomes a soap opera and begins

to get on everybody's nerves. The decision "will he drive or won't he" is taken in Brazil, for example, only on the Wednesday before the race. That Senna nevertheless wins, just as two weeks later, with that brilliant performance at Donington, he completely outclasses top favourite Prost in the Williams, shows that he is still able to maintain his concentration.

The climax comes at Imola: Senna arrives at the last minute, turning up in the paddock just 3 minutes before the start of practice on the Friday morning — after a 12-hour overnight flight from Brazil. When, after a few laps, he promptly goes into a spin, then does the same in the afternoon during the qualifying laps, there is no shortage of malicious tongues: "That's what happens if you haven't had enough sleep." But Senna defends himself: "Certainly that wasn't the best preparation, but the spins have nothing to do with it. They're to do with a problem with our active suspension." But why the late arrival? This time it's nothing to do with the game of poker with Dennis, but above all with the battle for the Ford engines. Senna is trying for all he's worth to ensure that McLaren is put on an equal footing with Benetton and gets the latest refinement, the series VII engine. Strictly according to the existing arrangement that can happen only at Silverstone in July, but Ayrton keeps repeating: "Ford must grasp that ultimately they can become World Champions only with us, if at all, but not with Benetton. I also told them that I don't see any point carrying on

Ayrton and his close circle: his cousin Fabio Machado, fitness coach Josef Leberer and John Connor, who allocates the Marlboro money.

without the new engines." Senna is attempting to apply pressure by all means at his disposal, and the war is escalating. Benetton team chief Flavio Briatore tells everybody, whether they want to listen or not: "There's no chance of McLaren getting the engines now. And if Senna doesn't want to drive then he should stop." And he adds wickedly: "Who needs him now anyway?" Yet at the end of the summer he tries to get him on the phone, because he's thinking of recruiting him to Benetton. But by then Senna's contract with Williams for 1994 is in the bag.

However, before and during Imola it's all go. For a while it seems as though Ford has persuaded Benetton to give in, but then they back down again. The new engine, installed just in case in the McLaren during Friday night, has to be taken out again on the Saturday. Ayrton explains why he is driving after all, even in these changed circumstances: "Because I said to myself in the end that I'd only be doing Benetton a favour by not driving. By digging their heels in they would have achieved what they wanted – they would have eliminated me as an opponent."

Of course he enjoyed the euphoric hymns of praise after his

two fine victories in Brazil and Donington – and this also provided him with the motivation to continue. "I didn't read much of what was in the papers in Europe after Donington, because I flew straight back to Brazil," he said, "but there it was very nice..." Then, when he was offered a pile of copies from England and Italy, he leafed through them with interest and with a slight smile. To be able to win with inferior material, to show who is really the best, means a lot to him. "That really is an incredible feeling. It's not completely new for me, but very strong. A very, very strong feeling, very deep emotions."

And particularly so because they are victories against his arch-rival Alain Prost? He denies this: "That isn't a particularly positive part of my motivation. I don't get a good feeling from it. My main aim is to win, it doesn't matter against whom. To be as far ahead as possible... I would be in the same situation, I would have the same feelings, if it were anybody else."

One thing that certainly encourages him to continue is that his chances in the World

Senna's hands, which express so much...

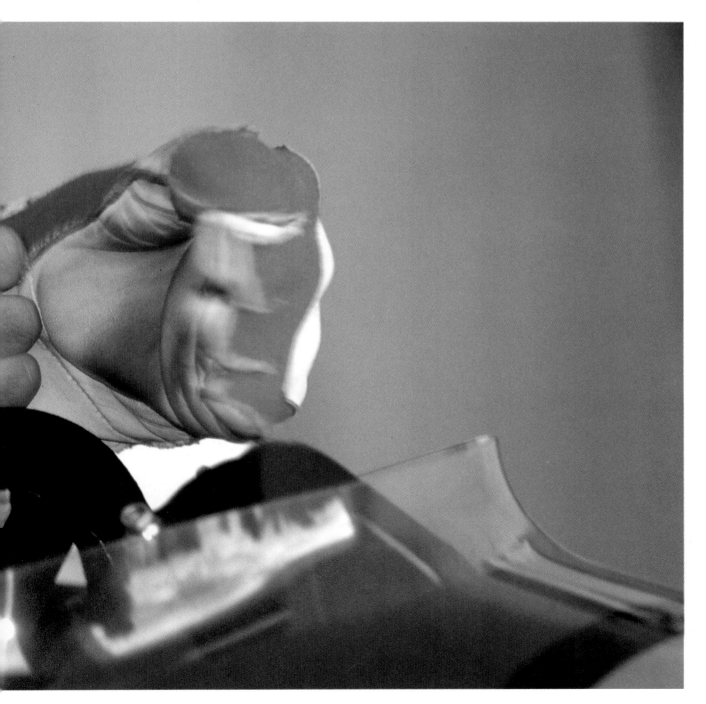

Championship do not, after all, look too bad. Admittedly he drops out at Imola, but then comes a second place in Barcelona, another win in Monaco and he's in the lead in the Championship when he comes to Canada. It's true there's still no contract, but most people don't pay any attention to that any more. At some point "the two pig-heads" are bound to end their "game of monopoly for real money", as the discussion has in the meantime been christened privately at McLaren. And didn't Senna indicate in Barcelona, if not earlier, that he assumes that he will be driving for the whole year?

But in Montreal McLaren lags hopelessly behind in the practice. Senna is stuck in eighth place in the line-up; he has not started so far down the field since the Austrian Grand Prix of 1986.

"I can only wait and see how the race develops," he says on the Saturday shortly before leaving just after 4 o'clock in the afternoon, which is quite unusual for him — usually he's discussing things with his engineers longer than all the other drivers. On Sunday morning he seems resigned, and in arranging an appointment for a story for the German Grand Prix he says pensively: "Who knows what will happen between now and then..."

"Does that mean you are again thinking of taking a break?" I ask him, and he just shrugs his shoulders. "I don't know, I have no idea how things should go on..."

But in the race the old battle spirit returns. The opening lap is very similar to Donington. From eighth position on the starting grid he immediately sprints up to fourth, then half a lap later he passes Gerhard Berger to move into third place. When Damon Hill, driving the second Williams, drops out ahead of him, a second place seems possible. But to complete a frustrating weekend Senna drops out with alternator trouble just eight laps from the finish. He is bitterly disappointed because he realizes he now has no real chance against Williams and Prost. Before the next race, the French Grand Prix, everything is on a knife-edge. Senna has been applying pressure everywhere: at Marlboro McLaren and at the American headquarters of the team's main sponsor, not just at their European office in Lausanne, through which negotiations are usually conducted. His argument is that even if the successes don't come, then at least the money should be right, as

money to Senna means first and foremost "a definition of one's own worth". But the word is that Ron Dennis also wants a definitive signature now, "otherwise Mika Häkkinen will drive..." – at least that's what he says.

The situation seems to be coming to a head. Senna is in Magny Cours, but he doesn't come to the circuit on the Thursday. "If I get into the car tomorrow morning, then it's for the rest of the season, otherwise no more for this year," he says on Thursday evening to a Brazilian friend.

On Friday morning, one hour before the start of practice, they finally agree terms. Even so, the contract will only be signed a week later at Silverstone.

Many people suspect that Dennis has given in over the money and that Senna in exchange has signed up for 1994 as well – especially as after Magny Cours he is always speaking of "building up the team, developing for the future". But they've got it all wrong, because by this time, in strict secrecy, negotiations with Williams for 1994 have already made a lot of progress. Senna knows that Prost cannot – and therefore will not – block him there for another year, so the Frenchman will be left with the choice of either accepting him as a team-mate or leaving. Frank Williams, who has always been a Senna fan, is understandably very keen to have his 'dream driver' in his team at last, not least because it will mean that Ayrton will no longer be a formidable opponent with the ability to make things so difficult for the Williams team.

But of course Ayrton will be saying nothing about all this for a long time yet, and at Silverstone he comments only that his greatest

Summer 93 in Montreal: "I don't know what will happen next!" ▷

goal at the moment is to find a way out of his frustratingly unsuccessful current situation. "And I will get out of it!" No details, but he sounds quite convinced.

For the moment he must wait, and that is hard for him. "It's not my strong point, I know that. Just as I know as a fact that I must have patience. I must learn to have patience. It's hard. It's very difficult, but I'm learning. I'm trying to live with this situation better and despite everything to make of myself a better driver and a better person. I'm trying to learn – but learning something like this is very hard."

What is striking is that a few years earlier he wouldn't have been able to handle such a situation so calmly; he would probably have become very difficult in his relations with other people and he would have become irritated by just about everything because of his frustration. "It's not that it doesn't make me mad now," he says of himself; "the feelings are there. The difference is that I can now control myself better and absorb much more than I show on the outside. Earlier, I simply let it all be expressed... Inside it still hurts me a lot. But, after all, it's my problem, not anybody else's. So I have to handle it better."

Josef Leberer, who spent more time with him than most people, is still amazed at Senna's attitude during this period: "Even in our close circle he didn't let go by taking out his frustration on us. There was none of that. And that made a big impression on me."

Perhaps his private hopes for Williams and 1994 help to sustain him. Because, if anything, things get steadily worse throughout the summer until his hopes for the current season have dwindled to just about zero. Prost's series of victories – from Montreal to Hockenheim he has four triumphs in a row – virtually decide the World Championship. For Senna, even winning individual races scarcely seems possible, and there is no more rain to assist him. The performance gap between McLaren and Williams hasn't got any smaller,

and for the time being even Benetton has clearly left McLaren behind: in the circumstances, Senna is hardly likely to beat Michael Schumacher.

Deep down inside Ayrton knows that he contributed to a certain extent to McLaren's 'summer crisis': "The fact that for the whole first half of the year, when I had no contract, I never did any testing certainly didn't help. It could be that we are now feeling the consequences a bit. But that's how things were. And anyway we could never really have posed a threat to Williams," he adds.

However, from mid-July he's available to McLaren once again for testing, and by September, after an inevitable time-lag, some clear signs of progress are to be seen at last...

But in the meantime he has to live with the extreme frustration of simply not being able to win, and to keep on motivating himself is difficult. "I can only try despite everything always to give my best, to know that I have achieved my own optimal performance – and to get my satisfaction from that."

He knows that if anything he is himself better than before: "I have the feeling that I am driving well, not making many mistakes. I am getting the best possible from the car and from the engine that is available to us. The results prove that. I have more experience, more balance than earlier, I know more about what I'm doing and how to do things in the best way. I am fully exploiting the potential of what we have. I am quite aware of that." Nevertheless, there are limits. In Spa, Jean Alesi just manages to squeeze him in the final practice from fourth down to fifth place. But Senna still has time; he could still counterattack with a 'mixed' set of tyres – those put under the least strain during the first two attempts

- so there is still just a tiny chance to win back a place on the second row. But he doesn't even try. "Not here, not on this circuit, where the risk is so extremely great, not for a fourth place. It's not worth it."

Ron Dennis, who in the meantime has at least the feeling that he's going to lose Senna at the end of the season, makes some pretty hard criticisms of his driver in a briefing for English journalists, accusing him of insufficient motivation and commitment. Although declared to be "off the record", the comments naturally reach Senna very quickly. He feels unfairly treated and is extremely annoyed. In Portugal, in the McLaren motorhome, there is a blazing row between him and Dennis as they vociferously vent their anger at each other. But that's the end of it, they don't wash their dirty linen in public, although in the first flush of anger Senna is certainly tempted to 'squeal'. After all the years with McLaren, both sides must have some mud to throw at each other, but in the end it's more important to him that he should have a peaceful and stylish parting from the team with which he became World Champion three times.

For it is while in Portugal that he states officially that he's going. When at the same time Prost announces that he will retire at the end of the season everybody knows it can only mean that Senna will be driving the Williams next year, even if the official announcement is delayed for two more weeks until October 11. Senna already seems to be immensely relieved and happy. He is sure of himself: the most difficult times are now behind him.

Two questions need to be put to him. The first is: "Last year in Australia, you said: `It is perhaps somehow predetermined that I won't drive next year.' Do you now have the feeling that some of the things which happened in 1993 were also perhaps predetermined?"

Answer: "That in the end I did have the opportunity to drive? And

some of the special circumstances that helped me in some races? Yes, I really believe they were."

And the second question: "With hindsight, what would it have cost you if you really hadn't raced in 1993?"

Answer: "A few wonderful victories – but perhaps above all the chance for the future, the chance to drive the Williams in 1994."

At Silverstone, Senna and Ron Dennis finally hammered out a contract for a season that was already half over.

"We are simply completely different"

The long-running feud with Alain Prost

They were always fighting: over the years the duel between Ayrton Senna and Alain Prost left more of a mark on Formula 1 than any other battle. It was a duel fought not only on the track – the conventional battle between two competitive racing drivers – but one which ran much deeper, being waged by two strong but very different personalities.

It was a battle for supremacy, for power, and above all for principles, a battle that was to have many repercussions and which would be stirred up and exploited again and again over a period of years...

Everything began in perfect harmony. When the new McLaren-Honda team for the 1988 season, comprising Prost and his new team-mate Senna, is presented to the press at Monza in 1987, Senna assumes the role of the model pupil who politely looks up to Prost as 'the great teacher'. "I have the greatest respect for Prost, not only as a driver, for his driving ability, but also for the way in which he gives himself, for everything that he has achieved."

But he knows very well that to achieve his own goal of becoming World Champion he must assert himself against Prost, he must

replace the double World Champion as the acknowledged number one in Formula 1. He has the self-confidence to do it, and as early as the winter tests he shows on many occasions who is the faster man in the team.

But the first races don't go as well as they could for Senna, and after the Mexican Grand Prix Prost is leading 3:1 on race victories. At this point it is already clear that the McLarens have such superiority that only Prost or Senna can become this year's World Champion. Already the World Championship has been reduced to a contest between the two team-mates, to a duel between the young pretender who is game for almost anything, and the established star who is no longer prepared to take the ultimate risk and who perhaps, because of his mentality and his attitude to racing, never was. This is a duel between two strong personalities who on the one hand are totally different, yet in many ways are much more similar to each other than either of them would care to admit.

But Senna does recognize some things in common: "The will to win is something that unites us," he says, only to add pensively: "But perhaps it's also something that divides us."

They meet and operate in an environment which is "in any case extremely unsuited to making friends", as Senna comments in the

In 1988 the world was still alright: Senna and Prost in conversation together with McLaren design engineer Gordon Murray.

summer of 1988, a summer during which he catches up with Prost, winning four times in a row at Silverstone, Hockenheim, Hungary and Spa. In Belgium, Prost seems resigned to the outcome and prematurely congratulates Senna on the title, giving the impression from the outside of being magnanimous and mature, a little bit above the whirl of events.

At first, only a few people notice how great an inner struggle he has, having to recognize and come to terms with the fact that here is somebody against whom under normal circumstances he can do very little with the same material, who time and again is beating him, especially in practice and qualifying, when it is a question of pure speed.

But four weeks later, in Portugal, the conflict surfaces for the first time in public. There had already been two abandoned starts, firstly because Andrea de Cesaris stalled, then because of a collision at the back of the mid-field. So there was yet another fresh start. Of course, Senna and Prost are on the front row as usual, but this time Prost, who, as he says himself, has "at last an absolutely perfect car again" is, exceptionally, in pole position. But although Prost steers into the middle of the track and squeezes Senna towards the outside, the Brazilian initially takes the lead.

But in Estoril Prost has the faster car, seemingly the better engine management and chassis set-ups and, unlike Senna, a fuel computer that is working properly. On the second lap he attacks, making a perfect exit from the final bend and aiming to pass Senna on the inside as they race down the start-finish straight. But Senna keeps on steering to the right, the space

Where the conflict began: the bitter duel between Prost and Senna at Estoril in 1988.

74

between the two McLarens narrowing as Prost's car edges ever closer to the pit wall, where alarmed mechanics in a lightning panic reaction pull their signal boards in. Then Prost's car is bumped slightly to the left by an undulation in the track, Senna is forced to give him a little more space, and Prost is finally past him and goes on to win, while Senna falls back to sixth place.

Furious discussions follow in the McLaren motorhome, where Alain makes his team-mate explain himself and afterwards tells the press what he said to him: "I didn't know that you want to become World Champion at any price. If you're ready to gamble your life for the title, then take it! In that case I renounce it, my life is worth more to me than being World Champion."

High emotions –- but others see things as being a little less dramatic than Prost makes out. Gerhard Berger looks at the incident again on the television and comes to the conclusion: "It wasn't that bad." McLaren's Gordon Murray says: "If it hadn't happened between two team-mates probably nobody would have found much fault with it."

FISA security chief Roland Bruynseraede at first finds no reason to intervene, either, but then probably somebody "at the top" demands action. So Senna is called before the sport's authorities and warned: "The next time there's a manoeuvre like that you'll get a black flag" – disqualification.

Senna, already bitterly disappointed because he can't understand why his car, with which he has been satisfied for the whole season, suddenly isn't running properly, defends himself by turning the tables: "After all, Prost twice forced me onto the grass after the start, and after the first fresh start he did it again." Which is true. "Because of him I almost flew off,

so it's only getting my own back if I do the same to him." It is a situation that crops up from time to time. Senna feels himself in the right and therefore justified in taking what he believes belongs to him. He calls it principles, justice, determination... Others call him self-centred, "a contrary child".

A little footnote: Five years later, at Donington in 1993, he twice drives right in front of Prost's car during the free practice. The privately voiced question as to

whether he really needs to play such games draws the outraged response: "But Prost did exactly the same to me three times!" The fact that he was unlucky because on the television monitors nobody had seen Prost do it, so that once again he appeared to be the only bad boy, he dismisses with a relatively aggressive "I don't care" – probably because in truth he does care: his public image is more important to him than he cares to admit.

Back to the incident in Portugal,

what particularly annoys him about it is that Prost has told everybody what had been said between them in private in the motorhome. The trust is now gone, the break in their relationship has occurred, even if it's glossed over again for the time being, especially after Suzuka, where Senna duly gets his world title and Prost once again plays the good loser – allowing himself to hope: "Perhaps it will now be easier for me to become World Champion again in 1989. I hope now that

Ayrton has his title that things will be a bit more relaxed, that he won't be so totally focussed on racing and success – and will make things a bit easier for me."

Niki Lauda doesn't believe it: "Senna is more likely to be even better in 1989, especially if he is more relaxed and has got less to be worried about." Neither is quite right – at least not for the next year.

In 1989 everything erupts again at Imola, only this time it is worse than ever, even if it's not really

noticed at first because everybody is still in a state of shock after Gerhard Berger's frightful fire at the Tamburello bend, from which he was lucky to escape relatively unscathed. The only thing which strikes people at first is that Prost, who came in second behind Senna at the finish, is absent from the obligatory winners' press conference of the first three because, off the record, "he is incredibly annoyed". The details trickle through only slowly.

Before the race there had been an agreement between the two McLaren drivers. Because they are still so superior to the competition and can virtually share out the victories, there is no need to take unnecessary risks, especially in the early stages. Therefore, whoever makes the better start should hold the lead without coming under attack from his team-mate. But for how long, and until what point? Until just before the first bend? Until *in* the first bend? Until *after* the first bend? That is the crux of a conflict which develops into much more than an argument about a normal racing situation. In the second start – after Berger's accident – Prost makes the better start and takes the lead. As he approaches the Tosa hairpin bend he imagines he's safe, that Senna won't attack; Prost has interpreted their agreement as meaning there will be no attacks until they're through the first bend, which sounds entirely logical.

Senna, of course, as he says later, understood it differently; that the agreement meant no attack while braking in the first bend, and according to his version of events he overtook Prost not actually in the Tosa bend but before it: "He got a bit slower on the straight, perhaps he got into the wrong gear, I don't know. Anyway, because I was in his slipstream I was distinctly faster on

77

the straight. Was I supposed to brake to stay behind him? I was beside him already before the braking point for the Tosa bend, and then I braked a little bit later as well. For me the actual overtaking wasn't in the bend, but before it. And so it had absolutely nothing to do with our agreement."

However, Prost is so annoyed that in chasing Senna he gets into a spin, after which he has no chance at all. He feels he has been deceived and is so frustrated that he even

threatens Ron Dennis that he will resign: "I've lost interest."

Dennis, understandably afraid of losing his 'dream-team', has a long conversation on the phone with Senna, who for a long time can't understand why Prost is making such an enormous fuss about the matter. Dennis asks him to apologize "so that the matter can be closed, so that we can carry on".

At first Ayrton doesn't want to: "In my opinion there was nothing to apologize for. But Ron put on a

lot of pressure and talked of acting in the interest of the team and all these things..."

In the end he lets himself be persuaded and agrees to back down from his principles. While testing on the small circuit at Pembrey, in Wales, things are brought out into the open in the presence of Dennis, and Senna apologizes to Prost. "Against my convictions, I retreated from what I really think. It was very hard for me. But I did it for the team and also

because I noticed what a state Alain was in." Senna fights – once again – with his emotions and wipes a tear away: "It hurt me to take the blame on myself unjustly, but it also hurt me to see Alain in this state." The conversation has no witnesses and Ron Dennis says in conclusion: "That's the end of the matter, and what was said here will remain between ourselves."

When Senna comes to Monaco two days later the headlines in the French sports newspaper *L'Équipe*

scream out at him: "Prost says: `Senna apologized to me in tears' and `I don't want to have anything more to do with him, he's not sincere'." Alain has spilled the beans to his French media connections – and has once again played a bit of politics.

Senna doesn't react officially, but says on a later occasion: "Since that day I wanted to have nothing more to do with him." When two weeks later in Mexico Prost tries to talk with him again, Senna gives him

the brush-off: he's "not interested."

The atmosphere is poisoned, and for the moment there is no going back. Josef Leberer is to recall later that he often felt like "taking the two of them, sitting them down at a table, and asking them whether they couldn't talk over problems like grown men." But then he has second thoughts: "I couldn't interfere just like that..." The only

Imola 1989: Senna is ahead of Prost, but the big question is, where did he overtake – before or in the first bend?

possibility is the occasional tense little joke. On one occasion, when the two of them are actually eating at the same table, Josef asks: "Is it safe to shut the door behind you without something happening?" "You'd better leave the door open," comes Prost's prompt reply.

Prost then declares at the French Grand Prix in Le Castellet that he will be leaving McLaren at the end of the year. Even before Monza, in September, he has signed up with Ferrari, joining Nigel Mansell there.

Meanwhile, in the 1989 World Championship Senna is still seen clearly to be the faster of the two, as in the previous year, but on several occasions when he is in the lead unfortunate mechanical problems force him out of the race, so that by the time they reach Hockenheim for the German Grand Prix Prost has a clear points lead.

But Ayrton perseveres, despite having to bear an additional personal burden of which hardly anyone else is aware. For some time

A sad victory for Ayrton at Hockenheim in 1989: his close friend and manager Armando Botelho has died during the weekend.

he has known that his close friend, father-figure and manager Armando Botelho has incurable liver cancer. Armando dies during the Hockenheim weekend, but nobody dares to tell Ayrton until the race is over. Only on the Sunday evening,

after his fourth win of the season, does McLaren co-owner Mansour Ojjeh take him aside in the TAG motorhome to break the sad news to him. As Senna goes from the paddock to his car to drive back to the hotel, he hides behind dark

sunglasses. He doesn't want anybody to see his tears.

He withdraws into himself even more than usual, speaks very little and tries to isolate himself – not only from Prost. But he is driving as well as ever and he finishes second in Hungary and wins again in Spa, so he is not lagging so far behind Prost; the World Championship is not yet lost.

Monza could be a turning point. But instead, Prost claims another victory because Senna, who had been holding a clear lead, drops out with engine trouble just a few laps before the finish. Afterwards, celebrating on the podium, the Frenchman throws his victor's cup into the crowd – well aware that in doing so he will both hurt and annoy McLaren chief Ron Dennis, who normally collects and displays all the trophies, and with whom Alain had enjoyed a close relationship before Senna joined the team. But Prost has been annoyed for the whole weekend and after

his win he launches into a massive attack on McLaren and Honda. He claims that he is constantly being disadvantaged, that he gets the poorer engines, that they don't want him to become World Champion because he's leaving the team. Honda responds with diagrams that show where Prost loses time against Senna, especially in practice: the difference is seen to be in the really fast bends – the places where it takes a particular type of guts. McLaren and Honda are clearly infuriated, but in Portugal two weeks later there is a joint press statement in which they try to paper over the discord with some well-chosen words: they had talked things through, they had assured Prost to his satisfaction that he always got equal treatment. Prost was said to regret the annoyance that his statements in Monza had caused. Such issues would in future be solved internally. It is quite a climb-down that they wring out of Prost, so for once the

politician has been beaten at his own game.

As the Formula 1 circus arrives in Japan at the end of October Senna still has a chance in the World Championship, but he would have to win in both Suzuka and Adelaide and he knows how difficult that will be. On the flight to Japan he spends a lot of time reading the Bible – his own personal way of finding strength. In Suzuka he faces an Alain Prost who is determined to resolve the World Championship issue here, to stake everything on this one race.

After an absolutely dream qualifying lap Senna is in pole position, as he had been in the deciding race of the 1988 World Championship. Moreover, this time he doesn't completely mess up the start, but nevertheless Prost gets away more briskly and takes the

The legendary crash at Suzuka in 1989, which clinches the World Championship for Prost – because Senna is subsequently to be disqualified.

lead. It is noticeable that in general cars starting from the left side of the grid get away better than those on the right, partly because they have a better line into the first corner. Gradually it begins to dawn on other people what has long been clear to Ayrton: that pole position is on the wrong side of the track at Suzuka. Not that this is much help to him now.

He begins his chase of Prost, knowing that come what may he has to win. But unfortunately he finds that Prost is driving his best race for a long time: aggressive from the start, full of determination and right on the limit.

Senna finds it difficult to put pressure on him and it takes him 40 laps before he is able to close right in on his tail. Even then he has problems because the configuration of the Suzuka track offers very few opportunities to overtake an opponent who is almost as fast as you are. Senna knows that his time is running out, so on the 47th lap he makes a big effort at the slow chicane before the start-finish line. "It was the only chance I had."

Prost had sworn before the start, as he later admitted: "I have often made room for him when it came to the crunch, in order to avoid an accident. But not today, today I'm going to hold out." For one thing, Prost knows that if they both leave the track he will be World Champion. He also knows that the chicane is quite well suited for something of the kind; it's very slow and therefore not particularly dangerous. As Senna tries to force Prost to let him squeeze past on the inside, Prost coolly steers against him and the two cars become entangled and skid to a halt. A camera shot from a helicopter reveals how early Prost has steered into the chicane; if one traces his trajectory further it ends up on the grass rather than on the track... As

the two cars come to a standstill at the side of the track Prost immediately climbs out. He's not particularly annoyed; after all, he's convinced that he's World Champion again. But Senna doesn't admit defeat that easily: he waves to the track marshals to give him a push, which is allowed under the current rules when a car has stopped "in a dangerous position". But who defines what is a dangerous place? The marshals push him – but in the direction of the emergency slip road, which means that he cannot rejoin the track at the point where he left it; instead, he rejoins beyond the chicane.

He drives to the pits, has his damaged front wing changed, rejoins the race and manages to win by overtaking Alessandro Nannini – at that very same chicane – shortly before the finish. At least, he thinks he's won. The shock comes just half an hour later: disqualification for missing out the chicane. "I really gained no advantage from it," he later insists, over and over again. The big question is to what extent FISA President Jean-Marie Balestre influenced the disqualification, which was, to say the least, a contentious decision. The sport's authorities who made it swear that Balestre was never with them, despite claims by other people to have seen and heard him there.

Senna is still sitting crying in the circuit management's tower when Prost cautiously comes through the door. He looks as though he wants to apologize. But Senna doesn't want to see him: "Please go!" He sees himself as the victim of a French intrigue which has robbed him of his victory and the possibility of winning the World Championship; robbed by Prost, who pushed him off the track. "Someone who shouldn't have been at that spot

slammed the door in my face. You shouldn't believe that from my words, just look at the video."

And, he believes, robbed by Balestre, who in his view forced his disqualification in order to secure the World Championship for a fellow Frenchman. McLaren doesn't accept the decision and lodges an appeal, in order to get their win at Suzuka restored. Officially it's nothing to do with the world title. "It makes absolutely no difference to us whether it's Prost or Senna." But any team would prefer the driver who is staying to be World Champion...

But Ron Dennis' "fight for justice" backfires, especially for Senna. However, Alain Prost really has nothing more to do with the strange ways of FISA justice. All he says on the Sunday evening in Suzuka is: "The problem with Senna is that he simply can't accept not winning. He can't live with somebody resisting his overtaking manoeuvres."

Obviously that was meant as a justification of his own action. But he's not the first person to have voiced similar feelings. Among others, Martin Brundle once said something similar – when they were competing with each other in the British Formula 3 Championship. And even if the comment is not directly appropriate to what happened at Suzuka, there may be more than a grain of truth in it. Because he knows that he is the best, it's very hard for Senna to accept that sometimes there are situations where he cannot show it.

But at some point Prost says something else: "Senna takes such risks because he has the problem that through his faith he considers himself invulnerable, immortal."

A pensive Senna in the summer of 1990:
he's still not really enjoying Formula 1.

The remark, whether or not it is deliberately aimed at Senna, hits the mark and has a long-term effect, much deeper and longer than any sporting clash. But it is not the only reason why Senna 'clams up' in the spring of 1990 when, after a long winter full of politics [which is a separate topic] Prost once again makes a tentative offer of peace. At the opening race of the season in Phoenix, Arizona, he offers his hand to Senna, but Senna ignores him: "I didn't have the feeling it was meant sincerely."

That is what is so important to him, what he sees as the fundamental principle of his life: sincerity, straightforwardness taken to its logical conclusion. Even good friends say of him: "He thinks very much in terms of black and white." He hates politics in every form. This is why he can't get on with Prost, who is the master of a number of tricks in this area and is skilled at playing people off against each other to his own advantage.

For half a year they ignore each other as much as possible. At many victors' press conferences Gerhard Berger sits, as it were, as a 'buffer' between them. But at Monza, Berger leaves early to catch his plane, which means that Senna and Prost – who are once again battling it out for the World Championship – remain alone to face the assembled press. Then an Italian journalist asks them both how long they intend carrying on like this; can't they at least treat each other like normal human beings?

For a moment there is silence, then Prost mumbles something like: "I tried in Phoenix, but if Senna is ready for it..."

Senna is bewildered for a moment, and then, after voicing a number of comments, he comes to

the conclusion that they don't really have much in common, "but all the same we both have a passion for the sport" and "if he really sincerely is ready to shake hands with me, then I'm ready, too".

It's a tight-rope act of small steps. Prost still wants to make his position clear: "There have been things which certainly weren't good, about which there are still different opinions, like Imola last year, for example." When he hears this Senna tenses up again and tries to suppress rising annoyance, but Prost gives way: "I think we should forget the last year. In my opinion, in purely sporting terms 1990 has developed fantastically, much better than last year. I had no worries about being in the front row with Senna here. I was sure nothing would happen. And also in human terms I have learnt something in this time. For motor racing, which has surely suffered a lot from our conflict, it would certainly be very nice if we could go through these last four races hand in hand."

Saying this he stretches his hand out to Senna and everybody holds their breath. But after a short hesitation, as though thinking for the last time "Do I really want to?", Ayrton goes for the handshake and subsequently there is even a demonstrative embrace between the two.

One who is particularly glad at the reconciliation is Josef Leberer: "I really like them both." But because they are such strong personalities, he added, it was so difficult for them to come together again, especially for Senna. "His distrust for Prost was so deep-rooted that he simply couldn't believe that Prost could sincerely mean anything he said about him. Therefore it was a giant step for Ayrton to shake hands with Alain. Such a handshake means a great deal to him, it's not the kind of thing he does lightly."

Josef believes in the peace, even if the stimulus for it came from outside. But the ice is still too thin to carry their weight, as will be seen six weeks later in Suzuka.

It's always Suzuka. This time the World Championship position is exactly the reverse of the previous year. This time it is Prost who needs a victory in order to keep open his chances of winning the title until the last race in Adelaide. If he doesn't win, Senna will automatically be World Champion for the second time.

The drama of the Suzuka weekend actually begins on the Wednesday: after the experience of the previous two years Senna goes to the authorities and asks for pole position to be moved from the inside to the outside, so that the driver who has earned pole position really has an advantage. Prost agrees, and the word from the officials is: "No problem, we'll do it."

On the Saturday Senna wins pole position by putting his last ounce of effort into the fight. Prost's Ferrari seems to go a little bit better than the McLaren, but once again Senna squeezes that vital bit of time, more out of himself than out of the car. He's delighted to have secured pole position because he knows it's very important to him. He knows that on Sunday he must win the start against Prost, for once the Ferrari gets ahead, it will be very difficult to overtake it again.

When he discovers on Saturday afternoon that the starting position will not be switched after all, that – so it's said – FISA President Balestre has voted against it in a phone call from Paris and that Prost, although only second quickest, will once again have the better starting position, his mood changes a lot. In place of the normal tension of a World Championship-deciding race comes swelling anger and rage. He has fought hard to record the

⌐ A 'reward' for the 100th Grand Prix: in Mexico in 1990 there's a cake from McLaren.

85

quickest qualifying time, taking every risk, only as it were to be punished for it. And, of course, once again he sees the interplay of the French Balestre-Prost axis. He feels deceived. His facial features become visibly harder, a certain amount of defiance comes into play. There's the comment which everybody who heard it remembers later: "Perhaps I will be World Champion tomorrow before the race is finished."

The idea that he could be sure of the title if he could somehow get rid of Prost, more or less the reverse of what happened in 1989, has occurred to everybody, of course, and various people indulge in amusing speculation about where and when the crash will come. The tension mounts among the drivers, too. When, during the briefing on Sunday morning, it is announced that this year drivers will be allowed to use the emergency exit from the

chicane if they skid off there, Senna gets up, furious, and walks out: that is exactly what he was disqualified for the previous year.

As he gets into the car a good half-hour before the start his face is a mask of stone – his eyes flashing only hardness and determination. What he is really thinking he admits, honestly and unadorned, only a year later, back in Suzuka, after he has won his third world title. "I said to myself, here I am,

trying to do my work honestly, and
I just get treated in an underhand
way. OK, if Prost wins the start
again, I will go for it." And then he
adds: "He'd better not try to pull in,
to get into the first bend first.
Because he won't make it... It was
the result of a wrong decsion
influenced by Balestre. I contributed
to it, but I am not responsible."

It's not exactly an admission that
he deliberately put Prost out of
action, but an explanation of what

the lawyers would call "mitigating
circumstances". And Prost, who of
course promptly manages a better
start, makes Senna's attack easy.
Instead of immediately moving over
to the inside to secure his trajectory,
he pulls left for a moment and for
fractions of a second opens a
window that — especially under the
circumstances — Senna is bound to
take as an invitation to "go for it".
He never really gets level with the
Ferrari, but then, when Prost really

**Suzuka the second time round: in 1990 the
accident makes Senna World Champion.
He was never quite level with Prost
before the first bend – a result of the
'wrong' starting position.**

does pull to the right on the
approach to the bend, Senna
doesn't pull back. They crash, both
of them ending up in the sand –
and Senna is World Champion.

Initially, as he returns to the pits
on foot, he's completely relaxed,

the tension has gone and he embraces Ron Dennis and his mechanics. At first there is just pure joy at the title, that the battle is over. Only during the course of the afternoon, as he is forced to keep facing the same question, as he feels himself once more to be in the crossfire of massive criticism, does his mood change. He is driven onto the defensive, speaks of "a normal racing accident", that the failure to change the starting position certainly played a part in it, and that the world title is always the result of an entire season, not of a single race. He repeats this line of reasoning time and time again, and is still doing so at 5 o'clock in the evening, surrounded by a crowd of reporters, as the sun slowly begins to set. "I don't care what Prost says," he insists, sticking to his own point of view, when he is confronted with Prost's accusations, and defiance makes his voice harder. "He's the one who took the risk. He must have known that I was on his inside. He made the mistake by closing the door on me. I can't be made responsible for his actions. I know what I am doing and what I can do – and I can live with it."

As we've said, everybody has to wait another year before the full truth emerges. Prost and Ferrari, of course, speak of a deliberate ram: "What happened in Monza was only hypocrisy, now he's shown his true character," explodes the Frenchman. "What a scandal, it's more than unsporting; what a bad example for the young drivers."

He, too, is full of emotion. Disappointment at the lost opportunity to take the title is part of it, and perhaps secretly he even asks himself the question which many ask: Why did he, the clever cool tactician, not give way at the first bend? He knew that he was bound to lose if there was an accident, but that he probably had the better car, and therefore all the time in the world to lie in wait for his chance. Also, he should have known Senna better than anybody else, his lack of compromise, his determination to dart into the tiniest gap, precisely in this kind of situation. Again, why hadn't he closed the 'hole' right from the start?

John Watson, the former Grand Prix driver turned television commentator, thinks he has an explanation. Prost had told him that he based his entire tactics on taking the first bend in fifth gear provided he won the start. "I knew I could do it in the Ferrari, but that Senna couldn't in the McLaren." Watson presumes that Prost was so set on implementing this plan that he could no longer change tactics and react in any other way when Senna was suddenly almost alongside him.

This is just part of a dispute among the experts which suddenly divides Formula 1 into a Senna camp and a Prost camp more sharply than ever before. Derek Warwick also thinks that Prost should have reckoned on Senna doing what he did and given way, while James Hunt attacks the Frenchman first for totally misreading the situation and now "grumbling like an old washer-woman". Niki Lauda and Jackie Stewart place full responsibility on Senna.

In Adelaide, at the last race of the season, which in World Championship terms is now rendered meaningless, emotions once more come to the boil. Senna states: "I lost my respect for Prost long ago."

Stewart and Senna really get in each other's hair in a television interview when Stewart accuses him of being involved in more incidents on the circuit than any World Champion before him. Prost, too, suddenly feels himself to be both unjustly criticized and misunderstood on all sides. He decides not to talk to anybody any more. People use the word "kindergarten", and most are agreed that it's a good thing that after Adelaide there are almost four months of winter break, time during which frayed nerves can begin to mend.

But, of course, the topic is still on the table when they meet again in Phoenix in March 1991. "We're just totally different, I go my way and he goes his," says Ayrton when one of the first questions of the new year is about his old adversary. And he adds: "I'm happy on my way. Whether he is too on his, I don't know." He even tries to make a joke of it: "Me, pick a quarrel with him? That wouldn't be right, he's far too small for that" – a reference to Prost's diminutive physical stature.

For a while it stops at that, with both of them studiously ignoring each other. There is no more open confrontation, largely because for a long time they don't get too close to each other on the track. The duel of the year is Senna versus Mansell, not Senna versus Prost, who never had any real chance of winning the title with Ferrari.

Meanwhile, Ayrton hints once again that for him the greatest problem in his relations with Prost is not what happened on the track, the accidents. What he can't forget, and what he believes he can never get over, are the personal jibes. In particular, the remarks about his faith hurt him deeply; he feels that he was made to look silly, and this is very painful to him, especially as he feels sure that Prost used this weapon very consciously and deliberately. "But I really don't want to talk any more about it. Only time can put all these things right and will eventually bring the truth to light."

Senna defiantly defending his first-corner tactics at Suzuka in 1990 – and the press try to record every word on the Sunday evening.

The impression that remains, and which keeps on coming to the fore in the years ahead, is that Prost can cope with the conflict better, also that he uses the clashes for his own ends, because he sees in them a political tool and doesn't let himself be so deeply affected by them emotionally.

The feud goes on: in Hockenheim, Prost feels himself to be blocked unfairly by Senna for laps on end. The Frenchman is faster in some places, but cannot overtake. Senna's cars can indeed sometimes become very wide, and never more so that when the opponent happens to be Prost. Then, uncharacteristically, Prost tries

a really aggressive move, gets it wrong and flies off the track – this time without having touched Senna's car – then afterwards grumbles intensely about his rival's driving: "The next time I'll put him out of action, I'll do everything to help Nigel Mansell to become World Champion this year."

Senna is equally furious afterwards, but mainly because for the second race in a row he has run out of fuel on the last lap. This time he has only a tired smile for Prost: "We know all about it, always he only complains about others, he never looks for his own mistakes. What he tried there could never work, on the contrary, it was not

without danger, he could have taken me with him... Admittedly, he was faster in a few places, but not where one can overtake."

Prost's outburst of rage in front of the French television cameras has consequences. The FISA steps in, and in Hungary at the next race the two squabblers are called in and presented with their punishment: Prost gets a suspended ban for one race because of his threats and Senna is issued with a warning over his way of driving. But what is seen to be almost more important: after the pronouncement of sentence, the two of them remain together in the FIA bus for a good hour, talking privately in an effort to clear up at

least a few of their basic problems. Meanwhile, a huge gathering of journalists and photographers has assembled outside the bus. Everybody smells a sensation, and when the two finally emerge, total chaos breaks out. In the crush, some people are almost forced to the ground, others are hit about the head with cameras, and furniture from neighbouring motorhomes is flying in all directions; all to catch the symbolic handshake and a few words.

But the words are pretty thin on the ground: "The conflict was a strain for us both, we've talked it over, it's better that way," says Prost. Senna speaks of "a new beginning", of their desire only to fight fairly on the track, but he still seems a bit cautious. One of his Brazilian journalist friends wants to know whether it could now really work. "We'll try," is his clipped answer. As we've already seen, a lot of their problems are really deep-rooted.

The difference between now and Monza in 1990 is that this time the 'reconciliation' hasn't come about from direct outside pressure. Nevertheless, many people have doubts about how long the peace will last.

It lasts until the autumn of 1992 – for the simple reason that Prost, having been dropped by Ferrari, is lacking a top car and so elects not to drive at all that season. But then Senna is forced to recognize that Prost has outplayed him and, not least because of his contacts at Renault, has secured for himself the coveted Williams cockpit for 1993 and furthermore has excluded Senna as a team-mate there. There it is again – Prost and his 'French connection', by which Senna time

and again has felt himself to have been tricked.

When, in Portugal, he finally learns that he's not getting his 'dream car', the Williams, Senna indulges once again in one of his famous emotional outbursts in which he says things that within a few minutes he realizes would have been better left unsaid. For example, his comment about "the racing car that can also be a weapon. It could be dangerous if we meet on the track next year." This could be perfect ammunition for his critics to use at the next incident, however small. The statement that Prost is a coward, "who wants to enter a 100-metre sprint as the only one wearing spikes against a bunch of opponents in lead shoes" is, on the other hand, simply amusing.

Fortunately, the 1993 season doesn't develop into a real duel. There are just a few tight battles, such as during the first laps at Imola and Silverstone, when Prost has a poor start and needs some time to get past Senna's McLaren, but otherwise they scarcely ever find themselves close to each other. Off the track there is the occasional ironic barb, like in Donington, but otherwise it is mainly total silence, a more or less mutual ignoring of each other.

Then comes that fine gesture on the victors' rostrum at Adelaide, the exchange of a few normal words at the go-kart meeting in the winter at Bercy, then a number of very fair comments by Prost on French television during his commentary on the 1994 Brazilian Grand Prix. And finally the last conversation at Imola – where it seemed as if movement towards each other was possible after all... A few days after the tragedy at Imola, Alain Prost perhaps sums it up most succinctly when he says: "Without the other one we wouldn't have been what we were, and are..."

1993 in South Africa: at least there is a brief handshake between the arch-rivals.

"You can't beat the system"

Struggles with the authorities – and the critics

A feature of Senna's career which is almost as persistent as the battle with Alain Prost – and which for a long time is inseparably bound up with it – is his battle with the sporting authorities, against what he perceives as "the injustice, the bad policies of Formula 1".

The major conflict begins in autumn 1989. Senna is already 'tuned in' to things as far as the understanding between Prost and Jean-Marie Balestre, the FIA and FISA President, is concerned. Hasn't Balestre said quite clearly on several occasions that he suspects Honda of disadvantaging Prost? And after the 1989 Portuguese Grand Prix, when Senna was knocked out of the race by Nigel Mansell [who was already facing disqualification, having been shown a black flag], didn't Balestre make the comment that "one can see from just this kind of situation that neither Mansell nor Senna reach Prost's level"?

Senna speaks of his hurt at the injustice: the Thursday press conference at Adelaide in 1989.

Even if not earlier, Senna is convinced after his disqualification at Suzuka – which in his eyes is absolutely unjustified – that he is fighting a battle on two fronts: not only on the track against Prost, but also off the track against the sporting authorities.

This conviction is reinforced by what happened at the appeal hearing secured by McLaren in Paris against the Suzuka decision. The situation, he decides, is really quite grotesque. The disqualification had been pronounced by FISA officials, in other words, by the representatives of the sporting authorities. The higher body which is now considering the appeal is the FIA, the International Automobile Federation, yet the President of both bodies is Jean-Marie Balestre!

What happened in Paris is also seen by neutral observers as a scandal. Suddenly it is no longer a question of the incidents in Suzuka, but in addition Senna is accused of all kinds of other things. He is confronted with a seven-point list of sins from the duel with Prost in Estoril in 1988, the accident with Berger and Patrese at the start of the 1989 Brazilian Grand Prix – for which the three drivers long ago privately agreed to share the blame equally – to Portugal 1989 and the incident with Mansell who'd already been disqualified... A whole range of incidents which, to say the least, are ambiguous... The authorities even stoop so low as to cite an incident from the French Grand Prix, when Senna broke a driveshaft at the start and tried to freewheel onto the verge as quickly as possible so that nobody would drive into him. Even that is now laid at his door as "dangerous driving"...

But quite separately from the substance of the charges, lawyers are agreed that the procedure itself is indefensible. A hearing must be conducted on the business for which it was arranged, not on quite separate matters. "It's as though you're in court for shoplifting and you suddenly get accused of murder," is Ron Dennis' striking analogy to describe what happened in Paris. The verdict is brutal. Not only is the Suzuka disqualification upheld – the World Championship thereby finally being decided in favour of Prost a few days before the Australian Grand Prix – but Senna additionally receives a fine of $100,000 and a suspended six-month ban for "persistent dangerous driving".

He is absolutely shattered – but he is determined to fight it. In Adelaide, on the Thursday afternoon before the race, he goes public and over a period of an hour and a half, almost without interruption, he gets everything off his chest, tears frequently welling in his eyes. He repeatedly asks for support in his "fight for justice. That's what it's about. Justice, honesty, those are important values in my life."

He has thought of throwing it all in, of not coming to Australia at all, or of giving up Formula 1 after Australia. "An enormous number of thoughts went through my head.

But first of all I am a professional, and I have a certain responsibility to my team as well, and to the sponsors. And secondly, I am a person to whom his own values are very important. So important that I won't let them be destroyed by other people. To run away is not my way. I will fight for my values and my rights."

And he asks the media for help: "You can't just watch while this sort of thing happens." What hurts him so much is that he feels himself

in the right and believes that all sensible and logical people must see things in the same way, yet he has the feeling that most people are on Prost's side. "I didn't cause the accident in Suzuka," he emphasizes again, "and you don't have to believe me. Just look at the video." He means the helicopter shots which Ron Dennis also keeps on showing, that demonstrate at what point Prost steered into the chicane... "I was never responsible for this accident, no more than for

After a long conflict Senna signs his driver's Super Licence for 1990 in Phoenix.

he thinks: "Everything that has happened has been to help Prost to get the title. The 1989 Formula 1 World Championship has been manipulated."

This is a comment that has repercussions. The fight goes on for the entire winter of 1989-90; Balestre sees red and wants a public apology from Senna, "otherwise he won't get a Super Licence for 1990". McLaren ponder for a long time whether they should take any further action against the FISA and FIA, but then decide against – partly under pressure from the sponsors. It was even debated whether to take the case to a civil court – which would probably have failed solely on the issue of competence.

In December, during the FIA World Championship award ceremony in Paris, there is supposed to be a discussion between Senna and Balestre. But the positions have hardened and the emotions are heated. Ayrton has no intention of withdrawing his accusations of manipulation or of apologizing. Balestre, well-known for his dictatorial, overbearing and intemperate behaviour, doesn't give an inch on his demands and also insists on the $100,000 fine. The two of them just shout at each other and absolutely nothing is achieved by the meeting...

Senna goes back to the sun in Brazil... Will he drive in 1990? Does he even want to? If so, will he be allowed to? The circus continues until mid-February. On the first list of starters for the 1990 season his name is missing: his nomination has not been accepted – because he has no Super Licence, because there has been no apology... The

many of the other incidents which they now want to blame me for. But I have been treated like a criminal, I've been accused of being likely to endanger others..."

Again and again he wipes the tears away: "I'm sure I have made mistakes, too, in my relations with the public and with the media. I haven't been open, I haven't been sufficiently accessible, sometimes I haven't made my position clear enough. But sometimes I couldn't do it, either, because circumstances

were against it. But sometimes it was quite simply wrong, too." He tries to make a new beginning: "Let's start again at the beginning, let's work better together. I will really try to do it better in future."

He is unusually open, honest and human. He lays bare all his vulnerability and hurt – and many who never particularly liked him are visibly moved. But he also shows all his rage and makes strong accusations against Jean-Marie Balestre; now he says openly what

$100,000 fine has meanwhile been quietly paid – by McLaren, with help from their main sponsor...

An hour later there is a new list, this time with Senna's name included. And there's also a fax, sent by Senna from São Paulo, in which he states that he had never wanted to claim that the 1989 World Championship had been manipulated, and that he apologizes if there were any misunderstandings...

Has he given in at the last moment? It almost seems so. But a year and a half later, in Suzuka in 1991, after winning his third World Championship, and after that 'near win' which he handed to Gerhard Berger on the last lap, he has that famous press conference where he settles some old scores. He says pretty clearly what he has previously hinted at only privately: that things had happened differently, not so straightforwardly, and not so honestly. "I did send a fax, but it said something different; this text that was published then was not mine..." Which permits one to come to only one conclusion: that there was manipulation again...

In any case, at the beginning of 1990 he still has no great enthusiasm for Formula 1: "It's only

out of responsibility to the team that I'm driving at all... So many people and their jobs depend on my decision, I have to think about that, too. But I feel empty, I don't have any feel for the car, for everything that is going on here," he says in Phoenix at the start of the season. The fact that he wins straight away doesn't change things.

Only in Brazil, when his fans offer him all their love and admiration, do things get better again: "That helped me to get back some of my motivation." But he suffers for a long time, partly because he still can't tell the whole truth, "otherwise it would have cost me my Licence," as he furiously comments in Suzuka in 1991. It's an outburst of pent-up emotions, of bottled-up bitterness, of great frustration, laced with lots of swearing – which is usually not his style at all. It's a case of letting off steam, of "now at last the truth must out", expressed aggressively, seemingly without regard to the consequences.

It was no coincidence that all this should have happened in Suzuka, apart from the symbolism of the place and the emotion of winning the World Championship for the third time: in October there had

been a change at the top in the sport's governing bodies when Balestre's place was taken by the English lawyer and former March Formula 1 team chief Max Mosley. And clearly, Senna has considerably more trust in him: "Max has the ability to empathize, he's intelligent and fair..."

But it is almost typical that his Suzuka 1991 outburst also has repercussions. Senna's statements, especially about what happened in the accident with Prost in Suzuka the previous year, get shortened and distorted. His statement: "I contributed to it, but I was not responsible", becomes in many reports a flat "I deliberately put him out of action!" Which he never said...

The British media in particular pounce with enthusiasm on Senna's rather explicit language, the freely used "four-letter words", and this in itself gives them something else to be indignant about. Ayrton tries to explain: "English is a foreign language for me, one uses particular words more easily than in one's mother tongue without thinking about the extent of the effect..." But this is something which the majority of the British media, who tend not to speak foreign languages, cannot appreciate...

Max Mosley is not very enthusiastic about the contents of the statement, either, because it shows the sporting authorities generally in a bad light. Mosley and Senna meet at the Tokyo Motor Show, and a little later, indirectly through McLaren, there is a statement from Senna to the effect that he regrets some of the things that were said in Suzuka; at the very least "the timing of the statement and the choice of words were not adequate..."

That this climb-down is entirely of his own initiative is doubtful, or at least, this is what he seems to be

The Adelaide press conference: "A humbling experience"

David Tremayne, in his book *Racers Apart* (MRP), recalls that he was amongst the cynical journalists who attended the Adelaide press conference in 1989 when Senna and McLaren chief Ron Dennis pleaded for fair play from the written media:

"The cynics, myself amongst them, had a field day. There was Ron Dennis, the man to whom only the electronic media seemed important, suddenly trying desperately hard to curry favour, to call up his good old written word troops in defence of justice. Yet at the same time there was nothing remotely amusing about the genuine tears welling all the while in Aryton's eyes. Nothing at all. I found it a deeply humbling experience to

see somebody so intense about a subject that they were prepared to open up their innermost feelings to a bunch of people, many of whom would probably use that frankness subsequently as something to throw back in his face."

And Tremayne went on to ask: "Is he the arrogant Ice Man? Or just a man so very vulnerable that he believes his only form of defence is to use the maelstrom of his own fearsome talent as a weapon for attack? Only time, that great quasher of causes celebre, may answer such questions with authority and, perhaps, determine precisely where this occasionally flawed genius, motor racing's philosopher king, deserves to be ranked among the all-time greats of the sport."

Speech bubble: Pô Sr. Balestre! Isso não vale!

Banner text: ISSO É O QUE ACONTECE NA FORMULA 1 COM O DITADOR BALES

hinting at privately a week later in Australia. Obviously, neither Mosley nor Dennis wanted any more fuss. "But forget it, I'm getting to the point where I don't care..." The battles are taking too much out of him, and it is beginning to look as though he can't be bothered any more...

Suzuka to Adelaide – for Senna this time window has a habit of attracting all kinds of annoyance, and it's the same in 1993. Despite a splendid win in Japan, Ayrton is really annoyed again, this time at the Northern Irish Grand Prix novice Eddie Irvine. Back to Suzuka: Irvine is fighting Damon Hill for fourth place and in doing so totally ignores

Senna's efforts to lap him, holding him back for several laps. Afterwards, Senna is incensed: "...in their fight the two of them almost drove into each other several times; Irvine was in the dirt a few times and threw up stones – and all right in front of me. How easily that could have cost me a certain victory; I could have gone off with them if something had gone wrong... In any case, I lost 15 seconds," he grumbles, "it's really not on." That Irvine, having finally given way to Senna, cheekily repassed him shortly before the end, was the final straw...

However, Senna calms down and that seems to be the end of the

The Brazilians make quite clear in Interlagos in 1990 what they think of Jean-Marie Balestre and FIA policies.

matter. But then the situation escalates – again through a series of unfortunate circumstances. Josef Leberer was right in the thick of it: "Ayrton was actually quite relaxed again. The recording of the race was being shown again on the television and he was making a few comments, 'look at the way those two are carrying on', but in quite a casual way... Then some sneaky person comes along and tips him

Suzuka in 1993: Irvine gets in Senna's way – an irritation that will have serious repercussions.

off about the crude comments that Irvine has just made about him: "Who does he think he is? F*** Senna!" Incidentally, the 'sneak' was apparently Senna's own PR lady Betise...

"Then Ayrton got really mad," says Josef; "that was simply very provocative. And one must bear in mind all the feelings and tensions that build up in a driver during a Grand Prix; it's probably impossible for a normal person to understand this. Stupidly, I was busy, with cooking or something, and when I turned round he'd already rushed out of the door..." Leberer is sure

that otherwise he would have been able to hold him back: "I would have told him to just sit down for a moment, have something to eat and in 10 minutes things will look different. If necessary I could have simply grabbed him. Perhaps he would have bawled me out or attacked me, but it wouldn't have mattered – our relationship is so good it wouldn't have been a problem. And in hindsight he would probably have been grateful."

Leberer says he can "certainly understand, but not approve" of Senna losing control after confronting Irvine in his team's premises, bearing in mind the Irishman's dismissive attitude, and then belting him one. "OK, Irvine probably carried on provoking him

– he was asking for it – but all the same, Ayrton put himself in the wrong and only weakened his own position."

As a footnote, the dialogue went something like this... Senna: "Don't you know the rules about how to behave when lapping?" Irvine, pointedly cool: "Let the other one pass!" Senna: "Then why didn't you?" Irvine, arrogantly: "Because you were so slow!" Senna: "How can I be slow when I catch up a whole lap on you?" Irvine continued to give provocative answers and, just before he stormed out, Senna gave in to his South American temperament...

"He is simply immensely emotional," Leberer says at the time, "which on the one hand is a

great asset, because he draws a great deal of his strength for brilliant performances – like this one in Suzuka – from this emotionalism. On the other side it is also his weak point – because others notice that they can strike him there, that he is relatively easy to provoke if you go about it in the right way." And if people can't get at him any other way they will try it on: "Especially the new young drivers have no kind of respect – just as earlier he didn't necessarily, either... Therefore Ayrton must learn to control his emotions better. Otherwise he just plays into his opponents' hands. I will certainly talk to him about it again in detail. To some extent one can practise this kind of thing, too..."

It is soon very clear to Senna himself that he made a mistake. "The use of violence is always the wrong solution," he confesses two weeks later in Adelaide, admittedly only to a small group of `neutral' French people, when once more he analyzes the incidents in Suzuka from his own perspective: "What made me so mad was not first of all that Irvine made a mistake. Everybody makes mistakes – I've made quite a few myself. That's not the point. What was decisive was that he was not prepared to accept even part of the responsibility. I was talking to a brick wall. He even tried to put the blame on me; I was in the wrong place at the wrong time, and things like that..." Still resolute in his sharp criticism, he nevertheless unambiguously apologizes for the attack: "My nerves were shot through – I'm very sorry about it. I don't want any controversies, any fights – even though sometimes one has to face them. I don't feel at all good about what happened. That I went and thumped him ruined my whole weekend, my victory."

Earlier, confronted by an international group which included many British people who had criticized him after Suzuka more strongly than anybody else and had shown absolutely no understanding, he had refused to speak about the matter, "because what I really say never comes across". Later during the weekend he launches another strong attack on the British media when he is convinced that they are just trying to provoke him again: "In any case, you have no idea...", he says dismissively. "Do you want `war' with them?", he is asked by someone else, and the answer is still heavy with emotion: "In any case they write only bad things about me. Now I've told them what I think, at least they've got a reason for it..."

On December 9 the Irvine affair is the subject of a hearing which both drivers have to attend at the FIA in Paris. Beforehand, Ayrton is sure he will be cleared, "but after a few minutes I noticed that everything was going the other way..." At the end there is a ban for two races, suspended for six months. His face reflects his anger as he comes out of the courtroom, his manager, lawyer Julian Jakobi, beside him. But for the time being he makes no comment – which is certainly for the best and which Jakobi had strongly advised him. "Then in the lift he let off steam – but by then we were alone," recalls Julian. "I always tried to make it clear to him that he shouldn't harm himself with too quick, spontaneous and emotional reactions..."

This time it works, and he hardly mentions the matter again, until a few weeks later he just comments that what he was particularly annoyed about was that "there was no word about what Irvine did on the track... Because that was really dangerous... And if something like that has no consequences it makes room for further incidents." And afterwards came the somewhat resigned remark: "If I've noticed something in all these years, it's that you can't beat the system."

He has no more illusions about it: "Either you simply conform and have things relatively easy, or you fight and must then also be prepared to live with the consequences."

In Portugal, in January, he meets Irvine during the Estoril tests. There is a short handshake, but no great conversation... When Eddie is banned for three races after the 1994 Brazilian Grand Prix, in which he was at least partially to blame for a huge crash involving four cars, there is no comment from Senna... But was he able to suppress a private grin?

"The greatest challenge"

Monaco, a special place

Monte Carlo, May 23, 1993, shortly before 5.30 in the evening: it's a historic moment, one that will go down in the history of motor racing. Ayrton Senna has just won the Monaco Grand Prix for the sixth time – and for the fifth time in a row.

Alongside him at the front of the royal box, which doubles as the victors' podium, stands Damon Hill, the son of the previous record holder Graham Hill, and he is one of the first to offer his congratulations: "My father would have been proud that it took someone like Senna to break his record." Ayrton, moved, thanks him without words, with just a short gesture that speaks volumes...

He is overwhelmed by emotion, as ever at his greatest moments, and incredibly happy. Monaco means so much to him, not because it is one of his European homes, but because nowhere else does he feel so many demands on himself as a

driver: "Monaco is a fantastic circuit, the greatest challenge of all. You're constantly very close to the limit, really the whole time, the whole weekend. Not just in the race, but from the very first practice lap on the Thursday morning. You are constantly on the edge, at the limit – and between being right at the limit and only half at the limit makes a difference of half a second per lap." And Monaco 1993 is not a race which he can necessarily expect to win. Only two weeks beforehand he said: "This being permanently at the limit, which is typical of Monaco, is a constant

challenge. To get through the whole weekend without mistakes, without damaging the car once, really not to make the least mistake, that's what it's all about. A single problem can affect the whole weekend."

Something of the kind promptly happens: there is a nasty incident on Thursday morning during the free practice when he crashes at high speed at the end of the start-finish straight. He slightly injures his thumb, but the psychological effect is far more serious because of the knowledge that the cause is a basic problem with the McLaren: an

active suspension system that doesn't work 100 per cent on extremely bumpy surfaces. "After the accident I lost the last little bit, the last per cent between 99 and 100," he admits on Sunday evening after his record win. "It was getting better all the time, but right up to the end of the weekend I never quite got back to the absolute maximum. My hand was still hurting... And every time that it hurts, you naturally think of the accident again."

Heading for a legendary victory: Monaco in 1993, Senna's sixth triumph in the Principality – a new record.

In Monte Carlo in 1993 Ayrton's new girlfriend Adriane Galisteu is with him at a Grand Prix for the first time.

Pensively, he comments: "Every time when you have a nasty accident it sets you back. You take a step back and it takes a little time to build yourself up again, to get back to the level you were on. That's why it's so important not to have any accidents – in order to be able to keep on going forward, without any steps back. But when it happens, when you have an accident, you're knocked back and you have to be extra careful that you don't immediately have a second accident. You have to be particularly attentive, climb slowly back to the maximum without another accident. Otherwise it's doubly hard to get back to your top level."

He tries to concentrate even more than usual: "Basically, the most important thing really is to be still more attentive, to put all your senses even more on a state of alert, in order to recognize in advance any situation that could lead to a new accident and to avert it. But it takes time – even at the end of the Monaco weekend I was probably still not quite at the level I was on when I began on Thursday. It was OK again only at the next race in Canada; then I was back at the limit."

But Senna's 99 per cent effort in 1993 is enough to complete the Monaco challenge victoriously. "As a circuit it is the greatest challenge in the whole World Championship

because you are driving relatively fast and there isn't the slightest room for a single mistake. Because there simply isn't any space. Monaco is demanding physically, because one bend follows the other, and psychologically, because you have to be so attentive, so precise the whole time. The walls form your limit. Sometimes you are only millimetres away from the walls when you're going really fast on the way into a bend and you think to yourself `this is it, now I'm going to catch on something', and you know if you do then you're going to bounce off against something else and then that can be a nasty accident... You have the feeling you're scraping the walls, constantly, in every bend. And that's what makes Monaco so fascinating for me: this circuit can push your own limits a lot further."

He knows before the start that his chances are not the best. Alain Prost in the Williams certainly has the better car and Michael Schumacher in the Benetton is still ahead of him, too. Not lacking in tactical skill, he lets everyone know beforehand how much he will be concentrating on a lightning start today – the only chance from the second row.... Is that what makes Alain Prost a bit nervous, so that he starts too early, which costs him a 10-second penalty? In the event, at the forced stop the Frenchman stalls his engine and loses so much time that he's no longer a threat.

That leaves Schumacher, who in the early stages builds up a lead of over 15 seconds. But as Ayrton explains afterwards, his tactic is "at the beginning to try to look after my tyres and in any case to drive right through without stopping – and hope that the others will have to change theirs." Michael probably would have had to: the Benetton pits were expecting Schumacher's tyre change at about the 35th lap – but he doesn't get that far. On the 32nd lap the Benetton's hydraulics fail and Senna takes the lead without a fight, and thereafter is never in any real danger of losing this Grand Prix. He can even afford a precautionary change of tyres on lap 50, "only in order to take really no risk – I had a big enough lead."

In the end the victory is not as dramatic as some of his other triumphs in Monaco – but it is enormously important because of the record. The only thing that goes wrong is when he wants to drive the lap of honour, as usual flying the Brazilian flag: the flag slips from its staff and flies off, and he is left driving through Monaco with an empty stick in his hand...

Monaco in 1993: the hand injured in the practice accident causes a few problems.

But that's no reason not to celebrate handsomely that evening. First of all there is the obligatory royal dinner at the Sporting Club, then a short visit to the posh restaurant Rampoldi, then a long night at "Jimmy's" – and Adriane is with him the whole time; it's his new girlfriend's first 'official' entry to the world of Formula 1...

He celebrates – but as he does so his 10 years at Monaco must surely be going through his head, those 10 years since 1984 and the day when the name Ayrton Senna was drawn to the attention of the world for the first time with that brilliant second place in the pouring rain in an inferior car. It was a performance that astonished the

experts, "and I myself knew then, once and for all: I can do it!" From 1987 onwards he dominated the Grand Prix in the Principality, "and every year was something quite special for me..."

In 1987 he wins for the first time with the Lotus, "my first win with the Honda engine, the first of a long, successful and very close partnership", and – something that hardly anybody remembers today – the first win of a Formula 1 car with active suspension: Lotus was already experimenting with this system. "Apart from that, it was the first time that a Brazilian had won in Monte Carlo; that was also very important for me." When he's driving home that evening on his

The first win at Monaco in 1987: Lotus race director Peter Warr is the victim of the champagne fight.

scooter from the victors' dinner with the Prince he's stopped by the police for not wearing a crash-helmet: a strict requirement in Monte Carlo. He even has to go to the police station – the new victor of Monaco still doesn't mean anything to the unrelenting officers.

In 1988 there was no win, but instead an extremely bitter defeat, one which nevertheless Senna recalls as "one of the most important moments in my career, a turning point". He has built up a commanding lead of almost a minute over his team-mate Alain Prost when Ron Dennis, his team chief, tells him over the radio he can afford to drive a bit more slowly, so as not to risk anything. But in driving "a bit more slowly" Senna loses his concentration: "I'd already had one or two slight knocks." Then, 12 laps before the

end, he crashes into the barrier at the entrance to the tunnel. "I had everything in this race: a car that could win, my own ability to win, the necessary lead. And I lost this chance – through my own mistake. That hurt me a lot."

After the accident he doesn't go back to the pits, but instead crawls straight home to his apartment; even the team doesn't know for a long time what really went wrong. "But this mistake was a good lesson; I've tried to draw conclusions from it, to learn for the future."

He is advised and treated by his sister Viviane, who is a psychologist, and in order to strengthen himself mentally he turns still more strongly to his faith, to the Bible, in order to find strength and answers. "This race was really a turning point in my life – and in the end it had so

many positive consequences which far outweigh the one bitter defeat. Perhaps, in the long term, 1988 was my most important Monaco weekend of all."

In 1989 he takes back the victory he gave away the previous year. "I definitely wanted to make good. The memory of 1988 was still very strong. Every time I went to my apartment, which was only 200 metres from the site of the accident, every time when I was driving in Monaco, I passed the spot and could still see the traces of the accident." Every time there's a stab in the heart: "I simply couldn't distance myself from it. And somehow during the 1989 weekend I still had it at the back of my mind. But I was able to suppress it sufficiently so that it didn't bother me any more, so that I could win."

He knows very well that he also

needs this win for the World Championship: "Things weren't particularly good, after all I'd lost the first race of the year in Brazil, thanks to a stupid accident in the first bend..." It was also not an easy weekend for another reason: never before has Senna been so keen to beat Alain Prost, to thoroughly humiliate him. It's the first race after their quarrel at Imola, "and he had said very bad things about me in those two weeks. In particular behind my back, what he said face to face to Ron Dennis and me was something different. It was bad, and I was really bugged. I wanted only one thing: to be ahead of him the whole weekend, all the time. And then to win." And he succeeds, despite gearbox problems, of which Prost is unaware, so doesn't even try to sustain his attack. From halfway through the race Senna has lost the

use of first and second gears, "but I had a big lead and in other places I attacked very hard in order to make up for the time that I lost in the slow corners. In this way the gap remained more or less constant and he never noticed that I had a problem. This victory was the best answer I could give him."

In 1990 comes Monaco victory number three – in a year during which it becomes clear very early on that the World Championship is going to develop into a contest between Senna in the McLaren and Prost in the Ferrari. "Every point counted, so it was a very important win for the World Championship and also for me – because I still had some problems with motivation after all the political aggro since Suzuka. It wasn't easy, either, because I had gearbox trouble again, not as bad as in 1989, but trouble all the same."

In 1991, with three wins from the first three races, he comes to the Principality as the hot favourite. "But I already knew then that our car was really not nearly as good, as superior as it looked, that the Williams cars were actually faster by now. Only it was quite difficult to convince the people who made decisions. We were on a winning streak..."

But he knows one thing as well – that the McLaren is pretty reliable, at least in comparison with the Williams at this stage. Therefore, he is banking on being able to build up his lead now, in the first part of the season, "in order to have a reserve later on that I can eat into. For it was clear to me that in the course of time the Williams would get more reliable." Monaco, therefore, provides him with the best opportunity to win again.

"But it wasn't an easy race, not

A typical view of the race in Monaco: the cars almost disappear between the crash-barriers.

at all, even if from the outside it may have looked safe. I had considerable gearbox problems again, I had to fight." Nevertheless, he has the time while driving to follow on the huge video screen the massive battle some way behind him between Alain Prost and Nigel Mansell in the harbour chicane with Mansell finally squeezing past. "It was amusing to watch."

But after the race his exhaustion is obvious. At the victors' press conference he is unusually lacking in concentration and allows himself to be distracted. The phones ringing in the press centre irritate him so much that several times he loses the thread of what he's saying and he gets annoyed. Two hours of absolute concentration between the walls of Monaco have taken their toll although, of course, he is extremely happy; he is getting closer to his dream of reaching Graham Hill's Monaco record of five wins. "This was the fourth, and if I manage to equal the record next year I would at least have more wins in a row than Hill." He already admits that he's thinking along these lines. If he sometimes says that statistics don't interest him, it's largely said with tongue in cheek. Anyone who claims to be always and everywhere the best would, in the final analysis, like to see it expressed to the world in figures as well...

But 1992 looks like breaking the series. The combination of Williams-Renault and Nigel Mansell seems to be unbeatable. Mansell has already won the first five races of the season and is clearly in the lead again at Monaco. But Senna is a strong second and fighting for

The last laps of Monaco in 1992: the duel between Senna and Mansell writes another page of motor-racing history.

every tenth of a second in order to keep the gap from growing too large: "I knew that my only chance was to keep as close as possible in case he got a problem. I had to hope for this opportunity, and I never gave up. I was always at the absolute limit. At the technical limit, the car's limit and also my own human limit."

Right at the beginning, at the first bend, he had pushed past Riccardo Patrese who had started ahead of him: "That was the first part of my plan. If I had been behind him as well I would never have had a chance." With a supreme effort he manages to contain the gap between himself and Mansell to about 20 seconds, but then during one lap he loses almost 10 seconds: "It was terribly frustrating. Michele Alboreto had gone into a spin in the narrow downhill section between Mirabeau and Loews and he was stopped in the middle of the road. I was next and just managed to stop with wheels locked maybe about half a metre from his car."

He can't do anything because the track is blocked and he must simply wait until Alboreto gets his car in gear again and makes room to let him past. "I sat there thinking it just can't be true, now I've perhaps lost any chance, even if Mansell gets a problem now, I'm so far behind... It wasn't easy after that to fight on fully, to put the last ounce of effort into driving again. But I did it."

And he's rewarded for his fighting spirit. During lap 70 Mansell has a problem. "I almost left the track in the tunnel, I suspect tyre damage," he announces over the radio. He comes into the pits and changes all four wheels – we never find out whether the problem was really tyres, rims or wheel-nuts – and when he returns to the track he's a good five seconds behind Senna. The following seven laps are

about to have the fans holding their breath.

Mansell's Williams is already the faster car overall, and on a new set of tyres it takes him only two laps to close the gap behind Senna. But in Monaco to catch up with an opponent and to overtake him are as different as chalk and cheese. Mansell could certainly drive three seconds a lap faster – but he simply can't get past the McLaren: "Sometimes I saw three cars in front of me," he said later.

But even Mansell, who rarely passes up an opportunity to moan whenever he sees injustice, has no complaints afterwards about unfair driving: "He did what from his

point of view he had to do... We were both way over the limit." Wherever Mansell wants to go, Senna is already there. He keeps the car mostly in the middle of the road, and offers no gap, not the slightest crack into which his opponent might have been able to squeeze. He is in control of Mansell, his own car and himself, although by now his tyres are pretty worn out and he's always in danger of sliding off his chosen line, even of hitting something. Gerhard Berger says later: "Nobody but Senna could have won this race under these circumstances. Anybody else would have made a mistake sometime."

Sad symbolism: Josef Leberer in Monaco in 1994.

Senna makes no mistakes – and Mansell doesn't make any rash move to force the situation, as many expect. When the finishing flag comes down after the 78th lap the two of them are separated by just 0.215 of a second. This is just a blink of an eyelid, but it means the world to Senna. "Monaco is the most important Grand Prix of all. That's why it's so particularly great to have equalled Hill's record here. For me it's one of the greatest things that can be achieved in motor racing."

He enjoys his success, basking in the compliments and the applause which greet him everywhere, even when he comes into the press conference. He's there for almost an hour, and after the official part is concluded he willingly gives interviews in three different languages... Again and again he is thanked for interrupting Mansell's series of victories this year, which is beginning to bore a lot of people. He just smiles, quietly, a little bit dreamily, perhaps, because he knows he won't have many more chances to win this year. So he wants to make the most of it, to enjoy every second...

In 1993 he adds his sixth Monaco victory and his last dream is fulfilled, of having established his own record. The Principality of the Grimaldis finally becomes in motor racing terms the Kingdom of Ayrton Senna.

It's a brutal irony of fate that the first race after Imola in 1994 was to be held at Monte Carlo...

Farewell from his colleagues: before the start of the 1994 Monaco Grand Prix...

The absolute limit

Senna, the pole-position king

Of all Ayrton Senna's records, the one which is most likely to outlast the coming generations of racing drivers is his 65 pole positions from 161 Grand Prix races. For comparison, the driver who has come closest to this record was Jim Clark, who took part in 72 Grands Prix and set the fastest practice lap 33 times.

For Senna, pole position was never merely a means to an end, nor did it just mean the best starting position for the race. It was the expression of a Formula 1 discipline which he had made his own, the ability to consistently drive his car to the absolute limit, holding it on the knife-edge of adhesion, which he developed into an artform.

He could obtain as much satisfaction from a particular pole position as from winning the race

The lonely pursuit of pole position – Ayrton Senna's special discipline...

which followed it, and one of his finest efforts, which was certainly one of the most important for himself, was the one in Interlagos in 1991, when he achieved the seemingly impossible before his home audience – and afterwards tried to explain exactly how he could push himself to such a performance.

"I knew that the Williams cars were going to be a great challenge for me – and so they were: at their second attempt, they bettered my existing best time by half a second. In order to improve my own performance by at least the same time I had to do two things: to improve the car again technically – and to bring myself as a driver to an even higher level. Neither is simple when you've already at the first attempt reached a relatively high level."

The great improvement between the first and the second attempt, through the application of all the information gathered during the first run, was one of Senna's specialities...

On this Saturday in Interlagos, prior to making his second attempt he sits in the car for almost 20 minutes, practically motionless, his eyes fixed on the time monitor in front of him, a study of concentration. What is going on in his mind?

"The thoughts go along two tracks. There is a technical side and a psychological side. Technically I try to go through the whole last lap, what the car did in which bend, where it was good, where it was not so good. I think over possible modifications, discuss them with the engineers, we perhaps reject some ideas, and decide what we can do to the car."

In Interlagos he wants "firstly, purely on instinct, an aerodynamic modification", specifically an alteration to the wing setting. "The

engineers then checked on the computer whether it was possible and, perhaps helpful, the computer confirmed it and at the same time suggested a mechanical adjustment of – say – position X. Then I decided, again on instinct, on half of X."

But he knows very well from his experience that the necessary improvement of a half second will not come from these alterations alone.

"It's precisely when you have changed something on a car that was already good that you need even more mental strength to believe that you can also improve yourself. It's a question of believing in yourself, of the will to give everything."

He waits in the pits, strapped into the car, until the last possible moment. "Then, when I drive out of the pits, a million things shoot through my mind and body at a speed which you can't describe. Everything goes so insanely fast. So many situations – and reactions to them – come one after the other so quickly... It's a mixture of natural instinct and technical ability arising from experiences you've already made. They are models which can be recalled and according to which you act."

This particular pole position lap lasts 1 minute 16.392 seconds, 76 seconds full of tension and concentration at the absolute limit of human performance:

"It is an amazingly fast process going through your body and mind, all set for one goal, all focussed to one minor point, further ahead, something so far away that your eyes cannot see. It's really in your mind, projected there only."

As he comes back to the pits at the end of the lap, carried on a wave of cheering from the spectators, he sheds a few tears of joy, then he effusively thanks every

team member with a handshake, and the atmosphere is like after a great race victory...

Senna loved this challenge. A lap like this one in Interlagos was for him pure Formula 1, the search for the ultimate limit, which "when you reach it you realize that you can push it back a bit further..." This sprint, this lonely fight against the clock, in which he drew on "all my abilities, my experience, my instinct", came closest to his idea of "going to the limits", of "pushing the limits back", of "the search for absolute perfection".

In his last couple of years the Formula 1 rules removed a little bit of this fascination for him. No more extreme qualifying engines, as there had been with the turbos, and since 1992 no more qualifying tyres that gave extremely good roadholding, but really only for one lap:

"At that time it was a fantastic challenge, the greatest thing that you can imagine. Everything was concentrated on this one lap, and sometimes at particular places you held your breath for a long time just to drive fully at the limit. In a race of an hour and a half you can't do that. You're never in a position to exploit the full potential. But for 90 seconds, for one lap, the car can do it, the engine, the tyres – and yourself as a driver. That was something clear-cut – you, the car and nothing else. It was, to put it bluntly, the ultimate."

Without the qualifying tyres he didn't enjoy it nearly as much, and on more than one occasion he argued passionately for their reintroduction:

"They were abolished in order to make the practice safer, but that's not what happened at all. First of all there are now always far more cars on the circuit at the same time, so the risk of collision has not been reduced. For it's still the case that nobody is going to slow down

Concentration: on the times and positions of his opponents – and on his own lap to come.

entirely voluntarily on a fast lap if you catch up with somebody slower..."

It is a problem that has been rectified to some extent by the rule introduced in 1993 that nobody may drive more than 12 timed practice laps...

Senna's second argument: "You simply have much less grip, which means that if something happens, if you go into a spin, the car stops much more slowly. So the risk of accident is higher." And thirdly, this form of qualifying is much less attractive for the spectators, who can't follow what's happening: "Nobody really knows who is on a fast lap and when." But in the end, for him the main complaint was

simply that "now a lot that was special for the driver has been taken away."

He said this despite the fact that one of his deepest experiences in a Formula 1 car was at Monaco in 1988, when the short-duration qualifying tyres were not used. In the final practice he was improving more and more, driving each lap faster than the last until he was lying almost 2 seconds ahead of Alain Prost in the same car.

"I felt as though I was driving in a tunnel. The whole circuit became a tunnel... I had reached such a high level of concentration that it was as if the car and I had become one. Together we were at the maximum. I was giving the car

everything – and vice versa...

"Suddenly it was as though I woke up and noticed that I had somehow been on a different level of consciousness. I was really shocked, and I went straight back to the pits – and didn't drive any more that day. I realized that I had been in a kind of unending spiral. Faster and faster, closer and closer to perfection... But also more and more vulnerable, with less and less safety margin..."

This was an experience which was never repeated at that level of intensity – quite deliberately: "I didn't allow myself any more to go so far that I reached this state again. I can control it before it gets to this point. It's too risky."

Did fear – and commonsense – win over the lure of this sensation, or did he not sometimes want to experience it again? "Only if I could be sure that I would come out of it as I did then. But that's something I'm not sure of – that's why I don't really know, and hence the

Discussion with his engineers between two qualifying attempts: "What can we do to still improve?"

deliberate control…"

His 65 pole positions from 161 Grands Prix – they were the result of more than willpower, concentration, joy in perfection and sheer driving skill. Ayrton Senna developed his own particular strategies for this special Formula 1 discipline…

The perpetual complaint of all Formula 1 drivers: "I was held up on my fastest lap, I got stuck in the traffic," was hardly ever heard from Senna. It was not a matter of

chance – like no other driver he watched on the time monitor which of his rivals left the pits when, who must still have how many sets of tyres left, who must be exactly where.

"He took it in, analyzed it – and calculated precisely exactly when he should drive out of the pit road in order to encounter as little traffic as possible," explains Steve Nichols, his race engineer during his first years at McLaren.

And he took in little things that

nobody else noticed. In 1989, for example, most drivers complained that they had too little grip with their qualifying tyres through the first bends. Senna didn't have the problem; he had discovered that during their manufacture the tyres had acquired a kind of protective layer on top of the rubber – at that time Goodyear were using silicon to separate the tyre and the mould. So he concentrated on putting just enough stress on the tyres in the warm-up lap to clean off this layer –

without affecting the tyres themselves. Little details that went unnoticed by others – and he used them to his advantage.

For Formula 1 purists, for connoisseurs of the search for the art of perfection, Senna's pole position laps are a real treasure-house of unforgettable impressions, and the greatest of his 65 were also indelibly etched into his own memory.

The first, of course, was at Estoril in 1985, then there was certainly

Monaco in 1988, then the dream lap at Suzuka in 1989, and Monza in 1990 was also very important to him:

"There I hardly drove at all on the Saturday morning because of technical problems and I had to tune the car during the qualifying practice. Nobody expected that I would still manage to beat the Ferraris, but at the last moment I did it. That was really a great, very intense moment: I had given everything for this pole."

Then his 50th pole position came in Spain in 1990, but with mixed emotions following Martin Donnelly's dreadful accident; and Brazil in 1991, when he described in more detail than ever before what such a qualifying lap means. And of course Adelaide in 1993, for the farewell race for McLaren, his first pole position after a gap of a year and a half, which for him had been an interminably long time, and achieved under difficult conditions:

"I was trying in vain the whole time to talk with the pits to find out whether I had enough fuel for another lap. But my headset was jammed at 'on', or 'speak', so they couldn't give me an answer. But I didn't notice the problem, so while I was driving I was bellowing again and again into the microphone; I can't have actually been fully concentrating." Nevertheless, he was half a second faster than Prost in the Williams...

The last three, in 1994, he didn't find so exhilarating himself, not even the qualifier in Aida, which had looked incredibly good from the outside. But what had seemed so spectacular was for him not the optimum.

"Sure, it was a good lap," he said afterwards, "but not really great. The car is not yet in a state in which I can drive it as I would like to and how I could..."

'Magic' Senna

The search for absolute perfection

"Anyone who wants to beat him will have to reinvent motor racing!" This is a quote from Niki Lauda about Ayrton Senna which dates from the early summer of 1991, after the Brazilian had scored four impressive victories in a row, but the comment seemed equally valid through to the tragic end of his career. 'Magic' Senna originated in Portugal in 1985 – after his first Grand Prix win and the demonstration of how to drive in the rain in Estoril. And magic, with time, became just more and more magic, better and better, more and more perfect...

"Is Ayrton Senna the best racing driver of all time?" This question, asked so often, must probably remain without an objective answer, if only because with different times there can be no

Typical Senna: he would check every detail of his car, every day, before every practice...

basis for comparison. How can you rank a Fangio, a Clark or a Senna above, below or alongside each other?

What remains, and can remain, is the search for fascination, the analysis of what was particular to 'magic' Senna, of what it was that enchanted his fans and amazed the experts for a decade.

The perfectionism as a driver, his lightness of touch, the elegance of his style, this hint of supernatural genius: his fastest laps – and for him the best ones – were not spectacular in the normal sense. Not skewed across the track, no smoking tyres, not bouncing over the kerbstones, no wild feats of steering. They appeared controlled, on the one hand even calm, on the other somehow 'accelerated', as if a film was running a bit too fast. Especially when viewed from the car itself, recorded by an on-board camera. Also, this often showed that he managed with quite sparing, precise movements of the steering wheel, with no wild corrections...

Heinz-Harald Frentzen noticed, in the spring of 1994, during the tests at Imola: "If you watch very carefully in the chicane it's fascinating. Ayrton seems to guide the car through with two fingers; most of the others swing wildly all over the place."

As early as 1985, when Senna overtook him on a qualifying lap, John Watson thought: "Incredible, this lad must have six hands and six feet. I was flabbergasted..."

Less often seen than heard, another special feature of Senna's

At the limit, but not wild and spectacular: Senna had his very own style.

driving style was his sensitive use of the accelerator. He was constantly applying power and backing off with great frequency; it was a veritable tap dance on the pedal. In particular in slow and medium-fast bends, he used this technique to feel for the car's breakaway point, enabling him to bridge the time-lag between braking and accelerating, to feel earlier than others when he could accelerate hard again, and also to shorten the engine's response time. The result was that he came out of the bend faster. "It was in the slow sections that I lost the most time on him," says Gerhard Berger. "I did try to copy this technique, but I couldn't..." Alain Prost tried as well – with even less success. Senna himself never saw anything special in it: "I've always done it, I got used to doing it when I was go-kart racing at home in Brazil, it's normal for me." Berger's comment: "We others obviously don't have the sensitivity he has in his right foot."

Of course, electronic aids like traction control to some extent deprived Senna of these advantages – no wonder that he was critical of them. Just as he was critical in principle of the semi-automatic and partly programmable gearboxes: "For me, clean, precise and smooth gearchanges, at just the right point and as quick as possible, really belong to the art of the racing driver." He accepted that in the long term the semi-automatics helped the teams to "save costs, because over-revving and thereby damaging the engine is made less likely," but purely as a driver he was and remained opposed. "They level out driving ability." Incidentally, Senna never changed gear by ear, but always exactly according to the rev-counter, even in the thick of a crowded start or in heavy traffic when lapping. "Even in such situations he can always read the instruments precisely," noted an astonished Gerhard Berger on more than one occasion.

One of the secrets of his almost inevitable optimal starts... In 1993, at the crest of the wave of electronic aids, when most of the top teams already had fully-automatic starting programmes which just left the driver to step on the accelerator and steer, McLaren refused to instal one. "Ayrton starts better than any computer," explained Dr Udo Zucker, the boss of TAG, McLaren's electronics partner. The McLaren people also said at that time that while Michael Andretti in every situation usually kept slavishly to the pre-set gearbox programming for particular bends or combinations of bends, Senna often used the option of overriding the system and changing gear manually if he saw a way of doing better: "And usually it paid off..."

To pure technical driving skill one must add the mental component: "Even in technical discussions, he can maintain an extremely high level of concentration for a very long time, much longer than me," noted with astonishment Giorgio Ascanelli, his McLaren race engineer in 1992 and 1993; "often everybody else has to relax, switch off for a bit, but he can go on."

This is an ability which also distinguished Senna on the track: he had an even, very high level of concentration for the complete length of time required, whether for a qualifying lap or for the whole of a race. In three years together at McLaren, Gerhard Berger had excellent opportunities to make comparisons: "When I analyzed my laps, then sometimes I was 105 per cent in a bend, at the next perhaps only 90...

He was always constantly at 99 per cent – and the end result is faster. He never brakes too early,

never too late, he's never at the wrong angle..." The analysis of many of his 65 pole positions confirms it. Senna was not always the very fastest on every single section of the circuit – but overall he was. And usually he was fastest on the last part – which indicates two things. First of all, he was apparently able to distribute his tyre-wear so well that the tyres were still alright at the end of the lap, and secondly, his capacity to concentrate comes into play again: keeping the same high level – right to the end.

He had class which also showed in his racing: not necessarily driving the fastest lap – that wasn't his forte, especially in the last few years – but maintaining very fast and very consistent lap times for the whole distance certainly was. And in the lightning starts, with which he shocked his opponents on so many occasions: he made sure that during the first three or four laps, particularly in critical track conditions when all the others were still 'settling in', he showed them who was the boss...

Most of the others knew this, and at least grudgingly respected it. Over the years, in overtaking and especially in lapping, Senna built up a reputation for going about his business in a determined and uncompromising way: "I won very many races through it, and certainly lost one or two as well." This happened when one of the 'slow-coaches' reacted unexpectedly or a bit slowly, didn't notice in his rear-view mirror the yellow helmet flying towards him, suddenly made a mistake or closed a 'window' that was already open – and Senna could no longer take corrective action. Take the incidents with Schlesser in Monza in 1988 or with Nakajima in Brazil in 1990. "But this aggressiveness is part of my style of driving, a part of me – it always has

been. That's something you can't fundamentally alter. And, as I've said, I won a lot by means of it."

If he was extreme in his uncompromising attitude in the car, he was also extreme when it came to details. Saving weight wherever possible was one of his favourite topics. Even with petrol: if at the end of the race he still had 5 litres in the tank he liked to reproach the team gently: "That could have been calculated tighter and more exactly..." It was the same as with lapping: sometimes it went wrong.

That he twice ran out of fuel on the last lap – in England and in Germany – in 1991, and again in England in 1993, was certainly primarily a computer problem, but if he had not always insisted so much on reducing things to a minimum the technicians might have calculated the fuel requirement a little more generously, so that an error of 2 litres on the gauge would not have meant dropping out...

But he didn't like to have anything to do with such logic: "I don't want to give away the tiniest thing. Not in my driving – and not anywhere else."

He even considered whether it was possible to make his helmet lighter. Pierre van Ginneken, who latterly was his consultant at the helmet manufacturers Bell, revealed: "He made suggestions which might have enabled us to save parts weighing 5 grams. And he certainly didn't want to have too many layers on his disposable visors..."

He demanded progress towards absolute perfection of himself as much as from his partners. Bernard Dudot, chief of Renault's engines division, remembers to this day the first time he worked with Senna at Lotus-Renault in 1985 and 1986 – and his fascination and amazement at the time: "Once in Spa he

Over the years Senna developed a special partnership with Osamu Goto, head of Honda's engine division.

described to me for three-quarters of an hour a single practice lap, with all his impressions and feelings, but in particular all the technical data, rev-counts, oil pressure, etc. At every point, in every bend, absolutely precisely, going into the bend, in the middle of the bend and at the exit from the bend... Afterwards we compared it with the telemetry data – it was all exactly right. Incredible..."

One thing Dudot was quite clear about: "It can be just as demanding as it is fascinating for an engineer to work with Senna," he commented in the summer of 1993, when perhaps he already knew, or at least suspected, that there was going to be another

partnership between Senna and Renault. "For he demands as much perfection from others as he does from himself. And he's not necessarily satisfied with giving instructions about what should be done during long briefings. If in doubt, he stands behind you and checks whether it's really being done."

It was in engine development and fine-tuning, with his feel for the tiniest details, that he was ahead of everybody else. For Osamu Goto, chief of Honda's engine division in Senna's first years with McLaren, he was the ideal partner: "We were unable to work so well with any other driver; we didn't get such precise information from

anyone else, even about things which our computers couldn't tell us. Nobody took us so far forward – and we did have some other top drivers, like Piquet, Prost..."

In Estoril in 1993, during the free practice, he thought there was a problem with the engine: "There's a strange noise," he reported. But the engineers could find absolutely nothing in their telemetry data. There was some discussion: Should the engine be changed or not? At that particular time, with relations between Senna and Ron Dennis very strained and carrying over to affect at least some other people in the team, and with Mika Häkkinen as a new fast team-mate in place of Michael Andretti, there were some

The computer world of Formula 1 – for the drivers it means even more work.

critical voices. "He's got to have his say, putting on airs and graces because he's a star, annoying people," went the whispers. Finally, Ron Dennis decided himself: "We'll change it." And it turned out the camshaft was about to go; it would have lasted no more than three laps.

"He must have extra sensors in his body with which he feels things that others don't," Gérard Ducarouge, Lotus design engineer at the time, said as early as 1987. And he was ready to apply this extra knack, this gift, to take it to its logical conclusion, without regard for his own comfort.

"Many drivers have talent but are lazy. Others are workaholics, but have no talent. With Senna, everything comes together

perfectly: he has talent and a hardworking nature," is how Gerhard Berger summarizes the secret of his success and adds: "Hardly anyone really understood how hard Ayrton worked for his success, how much he gave. I experienced it and I learnt from him what it means to work in Formula 1."

The endless mass of data which the high-tech Formula 1 of the last few years produces – nobody could immerse himself for so long in the paper jungle of computer printouts, analyze every detail, evaluate it all for himself, store it in his head and keep it ready for recall in the future. Everything was subordinated to the one goal: to be the best, the number one – if possible always and everywhere. "Every free practice, every warm-up – whether

it was really important or not – he was really only satisfied when he was in the lead," recalls McLaren team co-ordinator Jo Ramirez. "He needed it. And sometimes in the qualifying practice after the first attempt he was so clearly ahead that really nobody could catch up with him. Then we didn't want to send him out again because we thought it was superfluous. But he insisted on driving again. Only for himself, in order to be able to do even better."

To be second was a defeat for him: "To be second is to be the first of the losers," he said. Only very rarely could he accept second place – and then only during the last few years: "In Monza in 1991," says Ramirez, "he was able to be happy with a second place because he

Senna and his coach Josef Leberer – for years they were very close friends...

understood that the points were decisive for the World Championship." It was during the second half of 1991 that the realization had grown that the World Championship could be won not only with victories. But he preferred to see it the other way: "If you win enough, the world titles come of their own accord."

He based the high expectations that he had of himself on the knowledge of his own strength, of his own ability, and on an unbelievably strong and unerring self-confidence which in turn made him even stronger. And on the knowledge of his own willpower, of his capacity in extreme situations to get a bit more out of himself – not only out of his body – especially for a victory. "Where he sometimes got

this strength from, what reserves he was able to mobilize, this incredible will, this is what fascinated me so much about him," says Josef Leberer. "He seemed to have no limits..."

"Every person has their own limits; perhaps mine are a bit higher," is a comment from Brazil in 1991, which was criticized by many, but was probably very close to the truth. A message from another world into which nobody could really follow him and which therefore cannot be subject to a final judgment.

Ayrton Senna – the best racing driver of all time? In the last year, in the last months, he himself felt that he was better than ever... "I have kept my basic speed, my style, but gained in experience, learned from

mistakes..." He didn't have the chance to show everything that he could have shown. He can't break any more records that would have been within his reach. "The little prince has gone back to the stars before he could conquer all," wrote Anne Giuntini in the *L'Équipe* magazine... But in any case, even the statistics would be only relative, would in the end not give an objective picture. So let's give up the search for an answer which can only be academic and ultimately contestable. Let's stick with the moments which 'magic' Senna conjured up in 10 years in Formula 1 out of every facet of his talent, his skill and his personality. They were far too fine to take away their magic through over-theoretical discussion...

123

"I have plenty of fear"

Confrontation with risk

Was it a premonition, or just coincidence? Two weeks before Imola, on the Sunday evening of the Pacific Grand Prix in Aida, Senna talked about the dangers of Formula 1 in considerable detail. Admittedly he was less concerned about the safety of the circuits or the cars than about the way in which, over the years, some of his colleagues had been behaving on the track.

Of course, he was very annoyed that Mika Häkkinen had rammed him from behind at the start. In Formula 1, he complained – first of all to race officials immediately after the accident and then by way of his interviews afterwards – at the present time there were too many young drivers "who thoughtlessly take risks that are too great". It wasn't simply that he had just been deprived by such an act of his chance of winning this particular race, but that "I am concerned that dangerous accidents are getting more frequent – and that we have no guarantee that everybody is

going to continue to escape without injury."

The previous year in Japan he had seen "three or four potential accidents" in the lapping business with Eddie Irvine, "then there was this nasty accident in Brazil, where it was only very good luck that nothing serious happened to anybody, and now here... I must say, when Larini – who could do absolutely nothing about it – drove into me I wasn't at all happy. If he had hit my car in a slightly different place..."

He talked about it for quite a long time, emphasizing that he didn't want any punishment for Häkkinen, "but this kind of thing must be noted, it must be made clear to the young drivers that there will be consequences if this kind of thing happens again. That's the only way to make them use their heads."

Senna didn't deny that earlier on, when he was beginning, he too made these sort of mistakes, "which perhaps led to critical situations. But what we need is for the boundaries to be established again so that the risks don't get out of hand."

Having grown more mature, and with the benefit of so much experience, he was increasingly concerned in his later years to reduce the dangers, although he recognized that the risk had an attractiveness of its very own: "As racing drivers we're used to living with danger. And the greater the danger, the greater the passion. And the fans, who love this sport, are also quite aware of this risk – the risk and the challenge. To some

"What happened?" – Senna in conversation with Formula 1 medical chief Dr Sid Watkins after Martin Donnelly's accident in Jerez in 1990.

extent they share our feelings and fears. I believe that through this they can learn and experience things that real life could never offer them."

Risk goes hand in hand with fear, which for him was never an alien concept: "Fear is self-protection; it stops you from going too far when you are at the limit. I have plenty of fear."

Very clearly he faced up to this after Martin Donnelly's accident in 1990 in Jerez. For much of that weekend it could be seen all too clearly how much this crash had affected him. "I was at the scene of the accident and it was very difficult for me to come to terms with it. Something like that shows your own vulnerability very clearly."

Why did he go there at all, why had he directly confronted the brutal reality? It's not an easy question and, even months later, his eyes glistened as he answered: "I went for myself," he said at the time. "Something like that can happen to any of us. I hadn't seen anything, didn't know how bad it

really was... knew that it must be bad. I only heard people saying all sorts of things; I noticed how many were going to pieces... I wanted to go and see the truth for myself. That's the best way for me: not just to listen to others. At that moment I couldn't do anything, but I thought if I was there, at the scene of the crash, then perhaps I could do something. You never know..."

Afterwards he crept away to the motorhome and was all alone for three-quarters of an hour, trying to sort things out in his own mind. "At first I really didn't want to go on driving." But then he went back to his car when the last eight minutes of the interrupted practice were resumed – and he drove his best time, a second faster than before.

"I didn't know in advance how fast – or slow – I would be." When he got back to the pits he was shaking and couldn't hold the tears back any longer: "But sometimes as a racing driver you have to be very hard on yourself."

"I will probably never be able to

describe the thoughts and feelings which I had when I got back into the car," he commented a day later, on the Saturday, after he had achieved the 50th pole position of his career; he was still shaken with emotions, fighting back the tears.

He had visited Donnelly in the medical centre at the circuit, but one thing hardly anybody knew: on Friday evening he had driven the 100 kilometres to Seville to visit him in the hospital there – and Donnelly, who had suffered severe head injuries and broken bones and was under very heavy sedation, had recognized him for a moment.

A year later at Hockenheim he went through a nightmare experience himself, the third in a series of nasty accidents within a few weeks.

First of all there had been his "holiday crash" while jet-skiing in Brazil, when he fell and a friend almost ran him down with his jet-ski, hitting him on the head. The result was a nasty laceration that needed 10 stitches.

A week later in Mexico he rolled

It was a miracle that anybody could still be alive: Donnelly's accident in the Lotus at Jerez in 1990.

his McLaren at the Peralta bend at 270km/h, a spectacular crash but without serious consequences. "I had to test my adrenalin levels," he joked later to his worried fitness coach, Josef Leberer.

And then came the accident at Hockenheim, just before 5.30pm on a Friday evening in the middle of July, shortly before the end of official testing in preparation for the German Grand Prix. "It was the worst accident in my whole career," he used to say later, "a very strong memory. I still know every detail; I remember every split second. I came to the first chicane at about 320km/h when I suddenly had a damaged tyre. I remember that I tried to spin the car round. If I had gone head-on into the tyre wall which at that time they still had at the chicane, I wouldn't have had a chance. But as soon as I hit the kerbs the car lifted and rolled over several times."

Moments and memories: a conversation in Australia a year and a half later. He still has difficulty suppressing his emotions as he tells the story; his eyes sometimes look into the distance as he tries to appear calm and collected: "I was at least 5 metres up in the air, as high as that palm-tree over there. And I also remember my helmet hitting the asphalt several times. I still know exactly what I thought and felt: I was sure I wouldn't get out. I was just waiting for the last blow."

There is real fear of death there, even if he tries to avoid the word. And the sure knowledge: "I know I was very lucky... But that kind of thing happens, it's a part of our profession. There is a risk that you can calculate and a risk that is beyond our control. And that's what happened here. This spot in Hockenheim – if you get a slow puncture there it's better to notice it at once and stop. Because if the

The emotions have a lasting effect during this weekend in Spain...

tyre loses all its air and finally goes it's almost bound to result in a bad accident. It's happened to me twice that a tyre has been losing air from a slow puncture and then finally disintegrated because of the high speed; the first time was in 1984 in the Toleman..."

The logical step for him was to fight with as much commitment as possible for track safety, and during the 1991 race-weekend in Germany Senna pressed several times for the piles of tyres to be removed from the chicanes, "which was very important for all of us. At first there was a certain resistance, but in the

end we were able to persuade the authorities that it was absolutely necessary, and it turned out to be a good decision. Also, the kerbs were altered in a few places, flattened so that the cars could no longer be thrown into the air like that; they did a few things to improve the surface of the track and then they enlarged the escape roads."

But his commitment to safety was not something he was able to maintain 100 per cent. In Australia in 1991, when the race literally drowned in the rain, he admitted afterwards: "It was a mistake that we started at all." He didn't make

In Mexico in 1991: the consequences of his jet-ski accident.

any attempt to organize a drivers' strike or to say resolutely that he for one would not start – above all because the manufacturers' World Championship was still in the balance for McLaren. He wasn't happy about it himself afterwards, and he tried to find explanations and excuses for his behaviour. The suggestion that really something always has to happen before the drivers will actually take any action simply drew a rather helpless: "I know, I know, but believe me, I couldn't act any other way" – not 100 per cent convincing, because he wasn't 100 per cent convinced himself.

Alain Prost took pleasure in accusing him of not caring about risks since he considered himself invulnerable because of his faith in God – a remark that hurt Senna deeply, "because that kind of thing is absolute rubbish. There is a great difference between faith and fear of injuring oneself or dying. Life is something that God gives us, but in most instances it is up to us to use our commonsense to show God that we understand that life and

health are a great gift from Him. It's our reponsibility to preserve such an important gift."

From most of his accidents he escaped unharmed, but in Mexico in 1992 he really hurt himself in a racing car for the first time. On the Friday, during the timed practice, the McLaren suddenly goes out of control on one of the many undulations and ends up hitting a wall; the suspension has been pushed through into the cockpit, injuring Senna's legs, especially the left one.

"I was in such pain I thought my legs were broken," he says later. The television pictures show his fear, his despair, his pain: his hands beating on his helmet in panic, then his face distorted by pain as the helpers remove his helmet, put a support collar round his neck and try to free him from the car. For minutes he's suspended in the cockpit, receiving oxygen.

Behind the pits his race engineer Giorgio Ascanelli is crying; the anxiety is tangible everywhere, so the relief is all the greater when the first reports come in. No spine

injuries, no broken bones, "only bruises and contusions" to his legs. It is March 20, the day before his 32nd birthday. Josef Leberer reassures anxious enquirers: "OK, he certainly won't be able to drive tomorrow, but basically there's no big problem."

And then he and Senna together manage the miracle of Mexico after all. On Friday, Ayrton too had seen no chance of being able to get into the car again that weekend. "The pain in the left leg was especially extreme, I couldn't move it or stand on it." Nevertheless, they try everything, "literally everything that you can do, for hours on end, even on Friday evening: lymph drainage, acupuncture, acupressure, massage, various ointments and constant ice-packs."

At midnight, for the first time Josef began to hope that "it might just work, perhaps he will be able to drive. But nevertheless we both slept for three hours before we continued."

Even after just those three hours' sleep, Senna later noted with amazement: "I felt much better, I even felt thoroughly rested, as though I had slept for 24 hours."

"Nonsense," grins Josef. "Later, early in the morning, when I treated him for another two hours, he was dropping off all the time." The special relationship that had been built between the two over the years, the absolute trust, is especially important in the course of this night. On Saturday morning, shortly before eight, Senna finally decides to have a try. "He has incredible willpower in such situations," explains Josef admiringly as the two of them arrive at the circuit just before 10am. But he's a bit proud of himself, too: "I can work incredibly well with him – and it's very nice when you can achieve something like this together."

Senna is still limping, and is visibly in pain when he walks and especially getting into the car. But what particularly bothers him in this situation is being pursued mercilessly by the cameras. He hates it when everyone sees him suffering, when he has no privacy even in moments when he has to show his weakness.

In the morning he drives for only a few laps "to see whether it will work at all". In the afternoon he drives the McLaren into the sixth starting position – as he admits – still in pain: "The vibrations are pretty bad. I've felt better on my birthday." But quickly he turns very serious:

"If it was just up to me, I wouldn't drive today. Firstly because I'm still in pain and secondly because I simply don't feel safe on this circuit."

His fury can be heard in his voice as he continues: "It's so unbelievably bumpy, worse than any city circuit. The cars are more in the air than on the ground. We come here year after year, every year they tell us it'll be better, they'll re-asphalt it, but it gets worse and worse. Every year there are more accidents. But somebody has got to injure themselves really badly or even die here before anything will be changed."

But he did drive... There we have it again, the compromise: he knows that something is not right and yet he goes on. Why?

"I am a professional, I have responsibility to the team as well, to the mechanics who stayed up till 3 o'clock in the morning building me a new car, to the sponsors and to the spectators – and so I definitely wanted to do it. If it had been my personal decision I wouldn't have driven, not for any money in the world. It's really not worth it to take this risk. Everyone is absolutely at the limit everywhere and it's only a matter of luck what happens when you fly off, whether or not the walls are far enough away, for example. And that really isn't acceptable."

He knew, too, in Imola in 1994 that the circuit was not as safe as it might be, that things could be improved.

He mentioned it as late as Friday afternoon...

Mexico 1992: the car doesn't look too bad – but Senna has hurt himself.

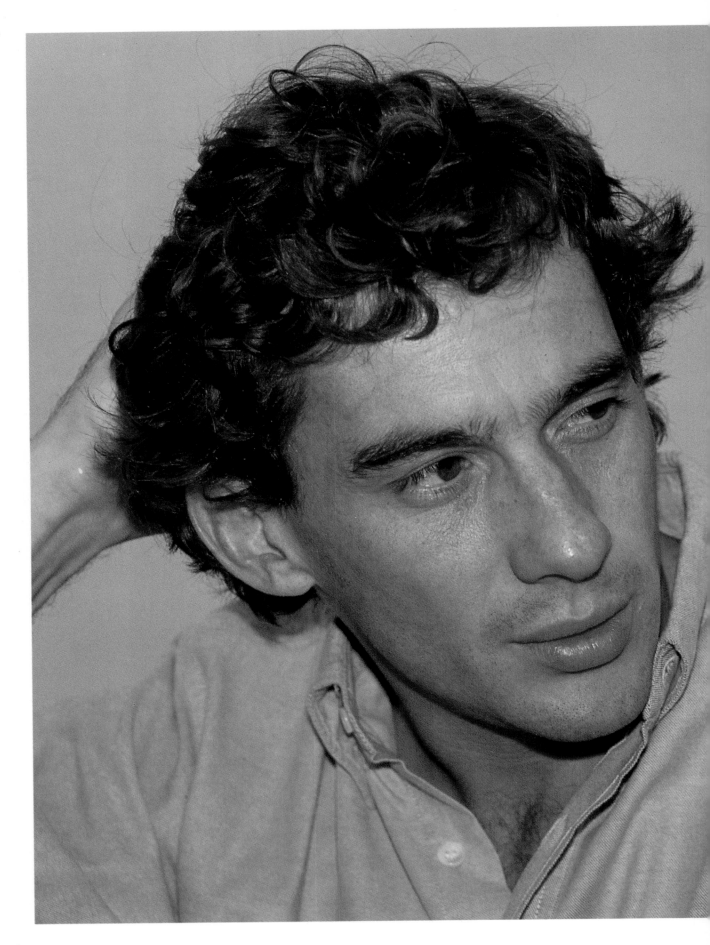

"God gives me the strength"

The complex link between world-class sport and religion

"God means everything to me. He is my support, wherever I am in the world. He is the difference between a member of the family and a friend. Belief in God in every situation everywhere has essential meaning. If you really believe then this faith is always with you."

Ayrton Senna and his deep faith, the source from which he got very much of his strength, for him the meaning of life – but for those around him often only a source of irritation and misunderstanding.

Religion, and especially Senna's tendency to give everything a somewhat metaphysical, mysterious touch, all this didn't fit with the clear, logical technical world of Formula 1, nor the very often similarly structured world of Formula 1 observers. He regarded himself as a very logical person and for himself personally he brought the two spheres completely together: "There is an area where one can apply logic and one where it doesn't work. Regardless of how far you have progressed on your path of experience and under-standing – there are simply things which you can't grasp with logic. And then you have to wait, have patience, believe that there will be a particular day, a particular moment when one will discover more, on a different level. OK, the sky is blue, that's green, something else is black – that's how we function. We tend to be able and to want to understand only what we can see, smell or feel. And if something lies beyond that, we think it's mad, nonsense."

But he himself has had experiences in which this "incomprehensible and invisible" suddenly became perceptible, almost tangible for him. "It was a fantastic opportunity, to experience this power, to be allowed to feel it."

There were visions, for example in Monaco in 1988, and especially also in Suzuka in 1988 as he took the last bends, as he was winning his first World Championship title. "I was thanking God for this victory, for this great gift, when I saw before me a huge picture of Jesus. It was incredible! I was actually still

driving with full concentration, with everything that I had – and yet there was suddenly this vision."

In Monaco in 1990, during the warm-up, "I could suddenly see myself from outside sitting in the car. Around the car and around my body there was a white line – like a wave. I saw strength and protection in it."

He looked for the answers to his problems in the Bible and also looked for help, "and I always opened the very pages that speak of courage, determination and strength." But how did he ever find his way onto this path, to these experiences? "The most important thing is to want to. That's the key. Life is not simple. Anybody can discover simple things. But not everybody reaches the more difficult things. That's what makes people different. Sometimes you have to stretch your hand out and take your chance."

He felt, however, that he had not made too much progress along this path himself: "I am still right at the beginning with my experiences. Like a baby. I know people who have got much further. They began just as I did. The beginning is the same for everybody. But then you have to go on. Sometimes something holds you back. Then you have to put more effort in and press on. It's not simple."

Words from the summer of 1993 – after a long period of time during which he had spoken only rarely on this subject. There was a time, especially in 1990 and the beginning of 1991, when he spoke relatively often about his faith, the meaning that God had for him, and he paid for this openness with ridicule, misunderstanding and ironic remarks from all sides. That hurt, "but it's something that is part of the reality of my life. I do believe that it's worth it to be so open: for the sake of those who want to understand and have a positive approach to what I say. Certainly many people use my words in a different way, even deliberately to hurt me. That's the price I pay, but I believe that ultimately the price that these people pay themselves is even higher. They just don't know it yet. It's difficult, sometimes unpleasant, to speak about such personal things. Neither is it always and everywhere the right place to speak about God. It's very critical, but I try to communicate to some people what I feel, what I experience, in the hope that they will understand it and value it. Whether or not I am right, everyone can make their own picture, but it should at least be respected."

He also wanted to give others the chance to find the way to faith, the way which had given him so much security, confidence and "inner freedom".

"It's really difficult to talk about it when you're in the public eye. You need to have the sincere wish to share such things with people who are perhaps looking for them and haven't found them. It's not my duty, my task – that's rubbish. In this special case I simply do what I feel. It comes from my heart. I know in advance that there will be people who will make fun of it – that's why they're here. But for me they are a minority and not worth thinking about. I know that such things happen, it hurts me terribly when some rubbish comes out that I never said, for example that I feel myself invulnerable or even immortal because of my faith. God gives me strength, that's what I said. But the others who listen properly are more important. Perhaps what I say can be a link in a chain for them, in their emotions, in their lives."

From time to time he tried to clear up some misunderstanding or other. It was known that he regularly used to pray before every start, "but I don't pray for victories, not for successes. I ask God to give me the strength to do the right thing and to do it as well as possible." Senna obviously also tried to explain with the help of his religious philosophy the conflicts that he was always getting into, to make them comprehensible to himself: "In the world in which we live, righteousness exists only through God's will. Human nature is of itself destructive, negative and envious. That's the role which the devil plays in the world: to incite people to robbery, crime and destruction."

But for him the negative was ultimately under control: "The devil is the real prince of this world, but everything that happens is determined and arranged that way by our King beforehand. It is sometimes really very hard for us to understand the ways that He has chosen. With our limited knowledge things seem good and right to us – but they aren't. Other things seem bad and wrong, but they aren't either. Everything has a reason, and God alone knows the harmony of the universe. His will, His reasons, His motives – He alone understands all that. Therefore it's my greatest wish to understand a bit better how He gave us life: the sky, the moon, the earth, the sun, the animals, man, the whole huge universe out there, unknown space of which we are still totally ignorant."

There's one memory that remains: a long glance of his into the starry sky of a tropical night over Australia, arising out of a really very relaxed mood, which suddenly became pensive. "It's a real miracle, isn't it, how it all always works, the moon, the stars, they are always on time and predictable, they never have problems – I find that fascinating..."

"I'd like to be able to see myself from outside"

A world star's philosophy of life

"If Alain Prost is the professor of Formula 1, then Ayrton Senna is its philosopher." That's how Canadian journalist Gerald Donaldson once described the two different characters. To listen to Senna, when he was in the mood to talk about more than his car, was just as fascinating as to watch his greatest victories and his fastest pole-position laps. And he was often in the mood – more and more in the last few years.

He liked to speak of his emotions: "What would life be without feelings?" he often said. He stood by his emotionalism and he tried to get others to share it: "There are simply emotions which only we drivers can feel. In our profession there are cars, team chiefs, the whole milieu, but the interest is focussed on us, the drivers. It's a very nice position, in

the centre of attention, but also very stressful, full of strain. Whether you win or lose, drive through a bend at a speed which a few seconds before you thought impossible, make a mistake, happiness, joy, annoyance, stress, enthusiasm, pain – only we and nobody else can experience these feelings and their intensity. In our profession we have a lot to do with ego. It's all about danger, our health, and it's second by second, not day by day, month by month or year by year. Our life is played out in seconds, even in thousandths of a second. It's a unique experience and position." So unique that he believed he couldn't communicate it despite his best efforts: "However much I try, it can't get close to what I really feel. You can't reproduce it, put it into words. In a way it's even like a drug. For in all these feelings

134

there is something so strong that it touches parts and systems of our brain and of our body that otherwise are never touched. And when it happens, the effect is so unique that afterwards you are always seeking it again."

He was aware of the intensity of the life that he led: "One thing which moulds our lives as racing drivers is that we do a great deal in a very short time. So we live very intensely. And when you live very intensely, then everything happens very fast. The difficulty is to do everything right, well, positively. For when so many things happen so rapidly it is very easily possible to make mistakes under all the pressure. That's the great challenge: to be nevertheless always good, positive and constructive. You don't always succeed, but it's the aim: always to do the best possible, to feel all the time that you're giving the maximum. For you are only at peace with yourself if you've done everything you could."

For him the search for perfection was a very important goal and the greatest motivation. "I believe everybody tries to give his best – in every profession, in life. Certainly we're all different and therefore act in different ways. There are no two people the same in the world. In such a performance-oriented environment as Formula 1, commitment and involvement count for a great deal. This will to total commitment, this dedication, either you have it or you don't. Certainly some have this will almost 100 per cent, others only 90 or 80 per cent. That's a question of character, of personality, of goals, of the desire to achieve something, belief in what you're doing, the will to fulfil your own expectations and dreams. That's different not only from person to person, but also from day to day."

Senna sought and found

harmony and his own kind of peace in perfection: "In the seconds before the start, when the engine is started, I let myself go, somehow let myself fall. All conscious thinking ceases, everything flows on quite naturally as though of its own accord. There is a rhythm, something like a perfect melody. Not always, but there is always the eternal search for it. When I find it then I drive in another dimension. Controlled, but totally free, steered only by my very own, I would almost say innate instincts. I am there in the present, but I am also ahead of myself and of time. I sense intuitively much more than I calculate. Unfortunately, these are only rare moments, but wonderful ones."

He was ready really to give himself totally for success. One day in the summer of 1991, when he was at a low-point with McLaren and any chance in the World Championship seemed to be vanishing, he admitted to me: "At the moment I am giving an awful lot of myself, the pressure, the effort, all this keeps on increasing during the racing weekend from Thursday to Sunday. Then you feel as though you are broken into little pieces, no longer a complete person; there are just fragments of a complete person left." He didn't know how long he could continue like that and commented: "It takes so much out of you, I simply can't regenerate any more during the season..."

Perhaps, he wondered, he should approach things differently. But immediately he rejected any such thought: "Because that just wouldn't be my way, my style."

Despite all the intensity he also knew the opposite – the feeling of emptiness. But he found ways of coping with it:

"I have experienced that a few times during my career and I have

also learnt from it, learnt to cope with it. One way of dealing with it is to do different things, to have different projects and to see how they develop. For then they became a motivation, a source of satisfaction and positive feelings. And you can transform that into energy in order to continue. You need plans for the future, things that you see gradually growing, that you can be glad about. If you don't have that and just wait for something to fall from heaven then it's much more difficult. And you need different things. Then if one thing isn't going so well you can turn to another one, and suddenly perhaps the first one will start working better again, too. You have to create new things and invest in the future. That's the only way to live for the future."

The future – that's what he wanted to live for. To live and to learn:

"Over time, as you get more mature and gradually learn to understand other people better, your own ability to handle other people also gets better. And when you try to improve yourself as a person, then time and experience can only help to bring out your strengths and suppress your weaknesses. The only way to improve yourself is to live, to live day by day and thereby to learn about living. And then you must have the right people around you, people who help you with the things you can't do yet, who stop you from making mistakes, who help you to learn. You can't do everything alone, you need people around you who make you stronger."

The aim of life, he believed, can only be to develop all the potential that one has in oneself. This is what he meant by "becoming a better person".

"Today, at 33, I am much closer

Pensive: Ayrton Senna, "the philosopher of Formula 1".

to it than I was at 20," he said in autumn 1993. "I am more experienced, more mature, tolerant and secure. I am very sure of myself and I am true to myself and my principles. Anyone who doesn't do that in our business is very quickly history and will very quickly be blown away by the others."

Many people considered him difficult, but how did he see himself?

"It depends. The key in any relationship, whether professional or purely human, is that you speak the same language, have the same basic values. Respect, trust, professionalism, competence. Then I'm an easy person. But if for any

reason something is missing, something fundamental – fairness, say, or honesty – then at once I become a difficult person."

Honesty and straightforwardness – when he didn't find those things he could never build trust. And if he didn't trust somebody they could never really get to know him. He became closed, he simply clammed up.

Even when he felt unjustly criticized he tended to do it: "It's hard to handle criticism when it is made publicly, and especially when it is destructive, when you know that it is meant only to destroy and nothing else. Then it is very hard to deal with it, almost impossible.

Then you have to fight, and I fight a lot. You have to accept constructive criticism. It is of fundamental importance to admit mistakes in order to make progress, to improve yourself. Part of that is accepting it when somebody points the finger at you, and makes it clear that you have made a mistake and why you made it. If you understand that, you can do better in future. But the problem is that human nature often wants only to destroy, especially when you are successful, a public figure. Then, for all sorts of reasons, people become envious and only try somehow to get their own back on you. Then you have to be very strong to deal with it. And that's why in the end there are conflicts. But that's how it is and therefore you must be strong and fight."

This doggedness was one of Ayrton Senna's greatest strengths, but he himself considered it to be sometimes a weakness: "Perhaps sometimes I should have given in sooner, perhaps even given up, changed tack, not fought things through to the logical conclusion. Some things would have perhaps been simpler then. But that's how I am: when I believe in something, I can't simply give up."

He was quite clear that this attitude kept on getting him into controversies. He took it on board – although he didn't want conflicts: "I don't like conflict, not at all. Of course, on the circuit there is competition, that's part of our challenge and that's OK. But I really don't like a fight which is carried on with words in a personal way. But nevertheless sometimes you're forced to defend yourself. Then you go public and the spiral continues."

In this respect he couldn't change his character, although he knew the negative consequences: "It's a pity, because a lot of energy is expended on it unnecessarily. What's more I've discovered that in things like that there are no winners."

Is that why off the track, in the spring of 1994, he tried to take all the sharpness out of the duel which was developing with Michael Schumacher? For example, he corrected questioners who spoke of "rivals" and suggested: "Can't we say 'competitors'?" It really looked as if in this respect, too, he was in the process of learning from experience and drawing conclusions from it.

There are an enormous number of questions which one could and would have liked to have asked – in the expectation of the typical 'Senna pause for thought', which sometimes lasted almost half a minute, and the well thought-out, precisely formulated answer which regularly followed, regardless of whether it was in Portuguese, his mother tongue, in Italian, or – as was mostly the case in the international world of Formula 1 – in English.

Almost always he considered very carefully what he said. The only exceptions were the occasional emotional outbursts, which quite often brought him trouble. And the answer was usually comprehensive, and not always easy to condense into a headline, so therefore the odd person occasionally forgot to listen.

But it was worth listening. In the winter of 1993, at the go-kart meeting in Bercy, I asked him to fill out for me one of those famous – or infamous – personality questionnaires, with fixed questions which can't be changed. I really didn't think he would agree, but he did, and the result was much more than the bare answers actually required. It became a long and sometimes very personal conversation, one which lasted for almost half an hour, and which until now has never been published in full...

What does happiness mean for you?
"Happiness comes from a state of mind and also from being at peace with yourself, being close to the people that you love so much, and besides that, doing what you enjoy doing."

What are your dreams about?
"Sometimes to do with racing, but more often about the many plans that I have at the back of my mind, things I would like to do in conjunction with my driving. Because I have had success through my driving I have access to lots of people, important people, who can have some influence in some projects that I would like to do in the future. And I dream of all those things, but nothing specific, you know, nothing particular. I dream about many different things I have done, some of the things I haven't done yet, just general things..."

What has really moved you recently?
"When I see a competition on the television, all kinds of achievements, a sporting activity when a man wins a challenge with other people, whether a single man or a team of people, I always get emotional because I know how important it is for sports people to achieve their challenge, their goals. I feel the same feelings so it touches me a lot... And this year, when I saw this meeting in Washington between Israel and the Palestinians, the meeting between the Prime Minister of Israel and Arafat. There is a historic conflict between two groups of people that has caused so much pain and bloodshed. Then you see those people being able to find the beginning for a new life, trying to put together peace among their people, it's all so touching. That was very much emotional, because we know how much they hate each other in many ways, what sort of conflict they had for generations, and it must take tremendous effort and goodwill to start some peace process."

What do you believe in?
"In God."

What do you consider your special strength to be?
"My direct approach to everything I do and my commitment and determination."

What is your worst habit?
"I sleep too much."

Do you have a dream for the future?
"Yes, I have. Some plans are still only in my head, I have still not found a way of starting them with other people. Others are under way, but are still secret [he had Senninha in mind], however you will know more about them in the next three or four months. But I have too many thoughts which I haven't figured out how to practically do it yet. When I'm lying in bed, in this state between waking and sleeping, then I can't stop thinking, thinking... I move from one thing to the next, and they become a dream, because I see them growing, progressing, happening, I see people happy about it... But then so far it is only a dream, it's not really happening yet..." [Supplementary question: Are these especially social projects for children?] "Yes, very much, not only with children, but especially for children."

What things annoy you?
"Corruption and lies."

If you could be somebody else, who would it be?
"Sometimes I wish I could be my little nephew, sometimes I wish I could be my father, with all his experience, or my sister, because we all have different activities, different responsibilities, and sometimes I would wish I could be a doctor, sometimes I don't wish to be anyone, just myself. But it is really just for the view, for the experience. Because normally I have a lot of attention from people who look after me, not letting other people come close. So I don't see many things that may happen around me, I simply don't see. And I know that some people treat me smiling and nicely in front of me and then, as I go away, they talk differently. And they don't treat people that are close to me as well as myself. And I often wish to be just an ordinary person, just to see how things really happen, being outside me to see how things are really happening, how people react, how they act..." [Supplementary question: As though you could fly above yourself?] "Yes, exactly [laughing]... Being able to fly, that's a great desire I have – but I don't think I will ever make it...

What strange habits do you have?
"I don't think I really have one. Maybe a habit is to enjoy excitement, I enjoy a lot exciting activities, exciting things. Maybe this is a habit..."

About whom are you able to laugh?
"About comedians."

What's your main characteristic?
"Never to give up."

What would you like to change in yourself?
"Perhaps to be able to accept easier how human beings are. It's difficult to accept certain things, but I wish in the future I can be more flexible towards people, accepting the way they are – some with their excellent qualities, some with their big flops. But the way they are."

What is it difficult for you to give up?
"Peaceful times – as well as excitement."

How do you over-indulge yourself?
"Just slow down, relax..."

What invention is the most important for you?
"I think the most important inventions all come from medicine. There were many, like the vaccines against polio, that was a great thing, and some other vaccines that came for all diseases that could now be fully controlled, that caused a lot of pain and stress before in a lot of lives. Technologically you can name many things, but they also proceed – you invent one thing, next year it's another thing, it's just progress. But really I think one thing we all, no matter where we live and how poor or rich we are, enjoy in a good way is medicine, is good medicine which prevents diseases and pain."

What ability would you like to have?
"Definitely to be able to understand other people better."

What illusion have you lost during your career?
"That no matter what you do, you cannot beat the system. So you have to make a choice. To be part of the system – or just to be yourself and cope with it the way it is."

Who is your favourite opponent?
"In different times of my career, different people. In go-kart times, it was Terry Fullerton... It was good fun. He was an excellent driver. In Formula 1, I would say Mansell and Alain..." *[Supplementary question: Not Gerhard Berger?]* "Not really, because Gerhard, although we competed, it was not in a negative way, it was in a good way, there was respect, there was understanding – so we never pushed each other to a very big, high limit. Because we always tried hard, but in a way never exceeded some limits, because he actually didn't want to make any harm to me, and nor did I. With

Prost and Mansell it was different; we were really opponents all the time, so we really pushed each other."

What disturbs you in sport?
"If things are handled in an unfair, incorrect way."

What person would you most like to meet?
"I would like to go back in time, to many different periods, not of my life, but of mankind. To the Seventies, Sixties, Fifties, Forties, 1900, 1800, 1500, the year before Jesus – and to meet all kind of people who made history or did good things. Just to be able to observe them, to see what they were really doing, why they were doing certain things, good things, not so good things. I think that would be the optimum thing to understand better life and human beings."

What headline would you like to read about yourself?
"Just my name – that's good enough."

What does popularity mean for you?
"Being popular means being liked by lots of people, being admired, as well as being the focus of stress and dislike and jealousy. Popularity means everything in many different ways. Of course, as anyone, I only enjoy the good things and don't enjoy the bad ones, but you have to be prepared to put up with everything that is part of being popular, having a public life."

What is the most stupid question you have ever been asked?
[He laughs] "I can't answer you without getting into trouble... But honestly, I don't really keep these things in mind. Especially in this time of my career. I am in a good mood, I am in a good spirit... I met here this weekend people from 15 years ago, from go-kart times. People whom I competed with, opponents I fought with, people from other factories, people who worked with me, who taught me a lot and whom I didn't see for many years, and I saw them all in a similar way. I didn't see the bad guys in a bad way then, honestly I didn't. You have to see the people... I was generally smiling to them, shaking their hands, talking to them about this weekend, about the old days, in the same way when I met the people I really liked then, that had helped me. I had a little bit better feeling, of course, because I had more identity with them. But generally I am only thinking good things. So I don't remember a bad question or a stupid

question, because it doesn't matter to me. It's not important."

Who or what would you like to take with you to a desert island?
"First of all I would go by myself to see the island, see what the atmosphere is like, then I would choose the right person, be it a friend or my girlfriend. It depends: desert island, what does it mean? Does it mean that you can be in peace, on your own, and meditate? Or does it mean that you can share with your love, with your girl? Or does it mean you can practice many activities, sports and so on, where you need partners, many people, not one or two? It depends how you see it, so first you have to go there and have a feeling for it, see what you really want to do there. But I don't think I would like to go with only one person. If it is a good place I would like to take quite a few people, that I like to have around me, to share things."

What hobbies do you have besides sports?
"Model aircraft, jet-skiing, water-skiing, music..."

Which sports disciplines do you consider unnecessary?
"None, all sports are good."

Your greatest disappointment in your career?
"As I said, I don't want to think negatively, so I don't want to remember such things."

Who is for you the greatest athlete of all time?
"Fangio is one, Pele is another, 'Magic' Johnson, Cassius Clay – if I think about it there are so many. They are all really great in their own way. I don't think you can name one above all because they all have their own strength, their own importance in my opinion."

What is worse than being defeated?
"Being cheated. Defeated, if it is in a sportive way, may be hard to take, but if you take it properly it can make you better. But if you are defeated because you are cheated, that's really unacceptable."

What is your aim in life?
"To live long and to be able to improve, and improve, and improve myself as the years come. Not only because of my profession, but because of my future life. Hopefully I can still do lots of things..."

"My upbringing is important to me"

Family and friends

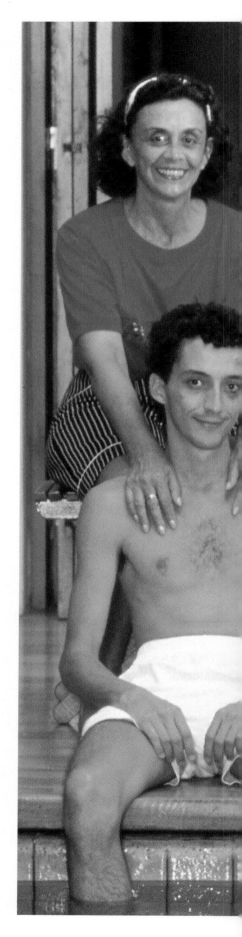

He lived all over the world and had homes in Monaco and Portugal – but Ayrton Senna was really at home only in Brazil: "Only there do I feel myself properly at home, that's where I have family and friends." Whether in his dream house at the beach at Angra dos Reis, on the coast between Rio and São Paulo, or on his farm Dois Lagos, near Tatui, 160 kilometres from São Paulo, with its own lake and go-kart track, or in his apartment in Jardims, a smart district of São Paulo – Brazil was his world. "When I go out just 10 minutes by boat from Angra to an island, to a lonely bay, alone, and just listen to the birds, that's fabulous..."

At such moments he loved to be alone, but sometimes he also suffered from it. "Loneliness is the price that I have to pay," he said, meaning the paradoxical loneliness in the midst of millions of fans, among strangers who wanted to get close to him, among the many apparent friends, of whom he was never sure: "Are they really thinking of me – or only the star?" For this reason he liked to withdraw into the most intimate circle, which consisted primarily of his family and a few close, mostly longstanding friends whom he really trusted.

His family: his father Milton, who had achieved a certain prosperity as an entrepreneur supplying the motor industry and as a landowner, but who was nevertheless very shy and reserved; his mother Neide, in public usually the 'grande dame'; his married sister Viviane with her three children, Bianca, Paula and Bruno; his brother Leonardo; and his cousin Fabio Machado with his three children – and in the last year,

At home with his mother Neide, his brother Leonardo and his father Milton – the family always gave Senna security.

The beach villa in Angra dos Reis – a refuge, especially during the Brazilian summer.

of course, his girlfriend Adriane belonged to this intimate circle. "When we were all together, then it was all go..."

He always wanted to have a family himself, to have children, whom he loved so much: "Children are natural, sincere and unspoilt. As an adult I often wish I could be carefree as a child again... And children are the future. If you want to change something, you have to begin with the children, with their upbringing..."

He could never refuse children. Even in moments of the greatest stress, just before practice or even on a race Sunday just before the start, he would never ignore a child who wanted an autograph or a photo. Once, during testing, when he knew that engine damage meant he would have a break of three hours, he suddenly disappeared in his own car... Afterwards it emerged that he had visited a boy in hospital who had had a serious accident on a moped and who, so he had heard, badly wanted to meet him. Senna refused

to make a big thing of it afterwards...

Allan, a British race marshal, and his son Mike, both of whom knew Senna from his early years in England, always came together to see him at the British Grand Prix. Then in 1990, when the father came to see him on his own, Senna immediately asked him why he was alone and discovered that there was quite a conflict in the family – the usual 'war of the generations'. When the son duly made his customary visit, again on his own, Senna spoke with the 17-year-old and urged him to think of his father's position for a change, to try to understand him, to look for a compromise, and perhaps now and then to learn something from the experience of his 'old man'. "It made quite an impression on Mike," recalls Allan, "and afterwards the two of us really did have a sensible conversation..."

Harmony in the family was an essential part of Senna's life, a part of himself, together with a certain respect for one's elders. In Brazil

especially, this respect is an important pillar of education, particularly with 'better' families. Senna was so deeply wedded to this principle that occasionally he had problems if others failed to show a similar attitude towards him – like Eddie Irvine...

He liked to remember his childhood and particular incidents: "When I was in the first year at school, my father promised me a bicycle if I got certain good grades. I wasn't an especially good pupil – but I managed it. So we went to a cycle shop and I was allowed to choose a bicycle for myself." What he wanted was "definitely a yellow one, I remember that quite clearly – and above all I remember how my father haggled over the price with the salesman for a good half-hour." It still made him laugh just to tell the story. "He was acting as though it was a helicopter that I wanted to buy. But I loved this bike. I had it for a very long time, long after it was really too small for me. But I didn't want a different one."

What his family gave him still

moulded him when he was a world star. "I had the good fortune to grow up in a very healthy environment, I had a very happy childhood, but I also picked up many values which mould my life and are important to me. My parents gave me a lot of freedom and let me learn from my own experience, but they also set the necessary limits.

"I am very proud of my upbringing, and I try to behave accordingly." His parents had always taught him, for example, that you should never ignore somebody, "so when somebody speaks to me I always try at least to give them a short polite answer..." In the stress of a Grand Prix weekend it couldn't always be kept up – but the willingness could be seen.

It was simply style and class, which shone through time and again, always and everywhere. Of today's Formula 1 drivers, who else would think of getting out of a taxi to open the door for a lady? Especially when he was going on further himself... For Senna it was quite natural...

Almost as important as the family were the few close friends. But even with them there were occasionally problems – when being in the public eye somehow or other got in the way.

The friendship with his childhood friend Junior, a close confidant who in the beginning often accompanied him to races, almost broke up under pressure from outside after Senna's rival Nelson Piquet spread about a few stupid remarks along the lines of "Senna doesn't like girls". It was only years later that Senna and Junior met again regularly, but even then with certain precautions: "If we go for a boat trip together we always have to take a couple of girls with us, otherwise somebody will take a

photo and the whole thing will start again," Ayrton once admitted to a close friend.

To Senna, his private life was sacred, and his great love for the Brazilian television star Xuxa broke up partly because Xuxa once talked a bit too much in public about their relationship; this kind of story was a nightmare. Other racing drivers may like to show off at having a different girl in tow every night in every different city, but Senna tended to be embarrassed if outsiders chanced upon such a story.

But there were a lot of things he simply couldn't stop. Then, shortly after his death, the story went the

rounds again that the Brazilian television starlet Marcella Prado had had a child by him. When the story had filled the front pages of the Brazilian gutter press for the first time in May 1993, his first reaction was both interesting and amusing: "Impossible! But if it's a boy, she can call him Alain..."

His friend Gerd Krämer, who teased him a few times about "his baby", once got a very serious lecture:

"If there was the slightest possibility that it was my child then I would have tests done at once. And if it was my child, then of course I would care for it. But there can't be anything in it..." Krämer's

Senna's sister Viviane – he often listened to her psychological advice

comment: "It wasn't even Marcella herself who kept on going to the press with this story, but her mother, who obviously wanted to push her daughter's popularity a bit."

Krämer, who had known him since 1984, was often his guest in Angra. "In 1993, we celebrated his birthday together on the boat, virtually on our own; none of the family were there. Once you were his friend, you were really his friend. Then he would do anything for you. For example, in the winter of 1993 he came to Stuttgart for the farewell for the Boss clothes chief Jochen Holy, just like that... And he always picked me up from Rio in his helicopter, he did this as a matter of course..."

He flew the helicopter himself, even before he officially had his licence. He secured his licence only in the winter of 1993-94 – "after I'd planned to take the test umpteen times, but it never worked out because I was too busy." In Brazil, nobody asks questions if you're called Ayrton Senna – and especially if you fly so well. His flying instructor remarked after a few hours' tuition: "I can't teach him anything more, he has an incredible feel for everything." But Gerd Krämer usually didn't feel "particularly comfortable" in helicopters, "I was always a bit uneasy. But when I flew with Ayrton, when we were flying among the islands near Angra, it was different. I felt quite safe with him."

In Angra he had the landing-pad right in front of the house, jutting out into the sea. It was a dream-house, mostly of wood and glass, 800 square metres, of which the living room took up 250 with its built-in swimming pool. Then there was the boathouse for toys like the motorboat, jet-skis, etc, and a gamesroom with table-tennis,

billiards and a giant video-screen and a super-stereo system for Senna the music fan.

Was this a dream world in the midst of a poor country plagued with problems? Perhaps, but Senna certainly didn't live in an ivory tower; he was well aware of the reality around him: "The main problem in Brazil is that the difference between the greater part of the population and a small part at the very top is getting bigger and bigger. For very many people there are no prospects, no future. I only see that things can't go on like that. In the long term the rich can't go on living on an island in a sea of poverty. We all breathe the same air... People must at least get a chance, a basic level of existence – food, medical care, education, training – otherwise nobody should be surprised that the problems get bigger and bigger and from time to time there's violence," he said once, referring to the problems of his homeland.

But he didn't have ready-made slogans: "I'm not a politician, I can't solve the problems." Senna never had ambitions to go into politics, like football star Pele, for example: "Because I believe that I couldn't give and achieve what I would have to achieve. At least at the present stage of my life I don't have the overview and the knowledge to achieve anything really good. And in my opinion you should only do something when you can do it really well. Otherwise, it's better to leave well alone!"

Anyway, he wasn't a great friend of politics: "I follow politics, one must do so because it directly affects the lives of all of us. But I don't like it. I don't like politics because I find it mostly dishonest. I consider myself an honest person and therefore it's hard for me to cope with the dishonesty in politics."

That didn't mean at all that the problems of Brazil in particular left him unmoved: "I see only that for the greater part of the population of Brazil things have been getting worse and worse in the past few years. That's a situation that depresses me a lot. That we can't do anything about it and at least give people some hope moves me very deeply – and makes me very concerned."

That he did a lot himself in the social sphere and supported charity projects, for example for the street children, was something he didn't like to talk about. There was always the fear that he would be accused of getting involved primarily for publicity purposes. "But there are a few opportunities to help various people in various ways. And whenever it's possible I do it."

Alongside this he also saw another way of doing something for Brazil:

"I think something that I can do for my country is that everywhere in the world I show my Brazilian flag when I win. And particularly in Brazil, an incredible number of people follow racing. They are very enthusiastic as far as Formula 1 is concerned – and everybody can watch on television, whether they are poor or rich. Even in the *favelas* [shanty towns] there is television, so everyone can be part of a Grand Prix when I'm driving. People identify with me, so all my battles, my successes, my victories are also a little bit their victories. And that does something for them... Amidst all the difficulties and violence in Brazil, every two weeks it gives them entertainment, an occasion to feel themselves a part of this other world, an occasion to be happy. I believe that it's important for people to have this sense of empathy and I feel that I have this link with them."

In addition he tried to

Among friends: Senna with Gerd Krämer of Mercedes and Boss chief Jochen Holy (on the left) in Heidelberg in 1992.

communicate to his fellow countrymen his own ideals and set of values that he was convinced of, such as commitment, dedication, straightforwardness, honesty: "I try in my interviews and sometimes even through my driving to show people these values, which I consider to be good and right, to convince them of them. Because I know that people are watching me, observing exactly what I do..."

Senna loved his country – and its people. Anybody who has observed him patiently giving autographs in the great hubbub of Interlagos, or, as he's leaving in the evening, waiting while his photograph is taken with all kinds of fans, is sometimes surprised at the image

of the cool, arrogant Senna which people in Europe liked to associate with him...

And the Brazilians had loved and admired him for a long time. When he won for the first time in Interlagos in 1991 and flew home from the circuit by helicopter to his parents' house in the north of São Paulo, a crowd of 5,000-6,000 people were already waiting for him. Josef Leberer was with him at the time: "There was an incredible mood, a crazy atmosphere, it was a great experience." When, after a considerable time, the crowd still didn't want to disperse, a compromise was worked out: "I'll come out onto the balcony once more with the cup," Senna offered,

"but then you must go!" It worked...

One of the secrets of this love was that Senna gave hope and confidence to Brazilians, and not just simple people. For them he was the proof that even in their crisis-ridden land, with all its corruption and injustice, it was possible to get to the top on one's own merit, keeping to the straight and narrow.

"He was our answer to the world which only ever saw in Brazil a country where nothing worked, that couldn't manage anything," Brazilians say. "What he did, through his victories on the race track, and also through his business success, was an encouragement for us."

"A challenge for the future"

Senna the businessman

"1994 will be the year in which the 'Ayrton Senna Group' will really become independent, from which all my business projects will develop their own existence independent of my career as a racing driver."

A sentence by Ayrton Senna from January 1994, full of pride at the mighty business empire that he had built up over the previous few years, from the creation of the Senna trademark, the famous 'Red S', to the general import contact with Audi – all of which will continue to exist without him...

During the winter of 1993-94 one of his favourite and often-repeated themes was "a project for children that we shall soon announce, in which I have invested

November 1993: Senna signs his general import contract with Audi chairman Franz-Josef Kortüm in Ingolstadt.

a lot, humanly and financially. But I believe and hope that it will do a lot for the children, and in the end also make money which can be put to other good causes."

He loved doing things a bit mysteriously – and in February he was immensely proud when he was able to show off the first issue of his new 'child'. *Senninha* was born, 'little Senna', a comic strip character who had a lot of himself in his make-up, even though he always liked to emphasize: "*Senninha* is not me!"

Senninha and his friends tell stories that are a mixture of reality and fantasy and, of course, they mostly take place on race tracks – understandably, the publication was an immediate and great success in Brazil.

The first issue, with a print-run of 3.5 million copies, was distributed free to schools and as a supplement with major Brazilian magazines. From March 15 there has been a new issue every two weeks "for about a dollar". That's no more than just enough to cover the production costs, said Senna, visibly proud of his project: "After all, everything's good quality, good paper, outstanding colour..."

It was not just a matter of offering children fun and entertainment, but also to do a bit of educating: "Through *Senninha* I would like to communicate something of my own values that are important to me: ethics, friendship, a healthy lifestyle, environmental awareness – and also simple things like correct behaviour in traffic." The *Senninha* character was conceived accordingly: "*Senninha* is a fan of modern technology, but nevertheless committed to preserving moral and emotional values, which are more and more often forgotten in our society," as Senna commented.

And there is another concept

behind *Senninha*: through it, various social projects should be financed. This works, for example, indirectly through advertisers: they can advertise in *Senninha*, and instead of paying high prices for the space they support all kinds of campaigns – at the beginning, for example, a project to distribute food to needy people. Additionally, there were spin-offs from the comic series: a computer game, a Walkman – with the proceeds from these going to a children's charity.

Senninha, it has been decided, will continue as planned: amongst the on-going projects are a 52-part television series with the *Senninha* character, probably also the planned film and short stories, and maybe also a launch in Japan, which has a huge market for comics and where Senna was still extremely popular from his time with Honda...

"Two years ago, the idea of doing something like this came up, we examined it, I liked it a lot – and now I'm proud that we were able to turn it into reality in this way," said Senna at the launch, "for this project contains a lot of myself and reflects my way of thinking and living." And for that very reason, says Senna manager Julian Jakobi today, "because so much of Ayrton himself went into *Senninha*, that's why *Senninha* must definitely continue..."

Julian Jakobi is the lawyer and manager who was Senna's consultant at the IMG management agency from 1986, who became vice-president and director of finance at IMG, and was recruited by Ayrton in the winter of 1991-92: "What he offered me was a great challenge both in business terms and personally. And the whole time that we worked together we understood each other very well and had absolute confidence in each other. That's a very important basis."

He also found Senna to be especially demanding intellectually: "He was one of the most intelligent people I have ever known. With him you couldn't take things easy. In his business life he was just as alert, attentive and quick with his reactions as on the racing track."

Jakobi was to develop the 'Ayrton Senna Group', which was officially founded on July 1, 1992, and to co-ordinate Senna activities worldwide from the London office. Besides the base in London and the Senna headquarters in São Paulo, where 'Ayrton Senna Promoçoes' and 'Ayrton Senna Licensing' were based, there were lots of things running in parallel: a partner firm, 'Ayrton Senna Promotions', in the Bahamas, a firm in the USA dealing with planes and travel, and the media consultancy work of Betise Assumpçao and the in-house photographer Norio Koike.

Betise not only co-ordinated press appointments, interviews, etc, she also made sure that the Brazilian media always got the right material. She sent her reports from the circuits to the office in São Paulo, from where they were immediately distributed to all the newspapers in collaboration with a Brazilian news agency.

Senna had already built up an information network of this kind in his early years in England, though of course on a smaller and simpler scale – but the principle was the same: "It works so well because the media know they can rely on it. They know that our reports are fair and objective." As a small service, for example, they always included a few items of information about the other Brazilian drivers...

I remember two visits, in the spring 1993 and the spring of 1994, to the headquarters of the Senna business empire in Brazil: a 16-storey office block, the Edificio

Senninha – his pride and joy.

victor's champagne bottle – "Detroit 1987" – and a helmet. "Our headquarters," says Fabio Machado, Senna's cousin and manager, clearly proud of the firm's offices. "We continue to work very closely with IMG" – Mark McCormack's sports marketing agency – "they support us in legal and financial matters, but ultimately everything is under our control."

The family always held the key positions in São Paulo: Ayrton's cousin Fabio, his father Milton and his 28-year-old brother Leonardo form the management team: "I must work with people I can trust absolutely," Senna always said, "and I find them best of all in my family." Julian Jakobi sort of belongs, too: "There is always a permanent exchange of ideas between us, we really work very closely together."

The division of labour at that time, in 1993, went like this: Fabio is primarily responsible for contracts and commercial matters. "I'm actually an engineer, but I worked for six years in the contract department of an American firm – so that's a good basis." Fabio joined the firm full-time in 1989 – after the death of Armando Botelho, Senna's first manager and closest friend. Leonardo's field is primarily promotion: "He gets around a lot, gets invited, goes to parties, listens a lot, knows lots of people, and lots of people know him. That's ideal to find new projects, to get new ideas. Additionally he's a computer specialist, which is often very useful, too."

His father Milton is primarily an adviser. Ayrton always gave a lot of weight to his opinion and experience – not for nothing did Milton quite often turn up in the early days at races in Europe when important decisions about renewing contracts or changing teams were

Vari, in Santana, in the north of São Paulo, with its own helicopter landing pad on the roof – after all, the boss wants to get to the office as quickly and efficiently as possible...

Seven storeys belong to the enterprise – and the first time I was there three and a half floors were being used, and the second time five, with further expansion being planned. At least 35 people were working for the Senna enterprises

in São Paulo alone – the majority of them quite young, and all seemingly very relaxed and happy. The friendly welcome there seemed refreshingly natural, not being at all artificial or contrived.

What is striking is that the styling is completely consistent, down to the Senna logo – the famous 'Red S' – on the office coffee cups. Unadulterated corporate identity! And everywhere photos of the boss, often signed for the employees, a to be made. Incidentally, it was he who was the very first to give enthusiastic support to the *Senninha* project...

The office in São Paulo also looked after the fans – a job for Fabio Machado's assistant Helena Nogueiro: "We try to support the fans and the fan clubs worldwide as well as possible. Of course, we get thousands of letters," she told me, "and Ayrton would like all of them to be kept. And he reads a lot of them, particularly the special ones which we select for him. And every letter gets answered, at least briefly." The affection of the fans was always important for Ayrton Senna: "Believe it or not, every present which he receives from his admirers at the racing circuits or elsewhere is kept."

But nevertheless, this side of things was not the most important. As we have seen, Senna was in the process of building up several projects for his future beyond his racing career – even though he wanted to drive for at least another three years and in financial terms would never have needed to do anything again afterwards. "But I could never do that, I always need new tasks, new challenges," he told me.

In his last major interview, which took place on the Friday evening at Imola, he laughed as he answered a question about why he inflicted this extra stress on himself: "Probably because I'm a bit mad," only to add more seriously: "But also, for instance, to secure the jobs of the people who work for me. If I didn't do anything else, I certainly wouldn't need some of them any more after my racing career. So I can take them on in other areas..."

And there was plenty to choose from: the motor trade, for example. In 1993 Senna secured the biggest Ford dealership in São Paulo, and the agreement which he concluded

The new fashion line – launched in spring 1994.

with Audi in November that year, which made him the general importer for Brazil, hit the headlines in Germany, too. A network of 15 to 20 Audi dealerships were intended to sell 600 cars in the first year – but Senna himself immediately raised the target: "We want to reach 1,000," he told the then Audi chief Franz-Josef Kortüm at the signing of the contract. In the first two months he took 160 orders – which were delivered in the first week of April... Incidentally, Senna had another business link with Germany from the late summer of 1993: Werner Heinz, from Trier, became his German representative and in Sonax secured him a private sponsor worth millions. "And other contracts are

on the table, just about ready to be signed; we were still negotiating on the Thursday in Imola."

Besides the motor trade, for some time there had been several licence projects, through which the Senna name was to be established as a proper trademark in the years to come. One of the first products with the Senna name to come onto the market was a motor yacht, 12 metres long and selling for $250,000. During the first two months after the unveiling of the project four of them were sold, even though immediate delivery could not yet be offered, and the sales target for 1994 was to be four a month! In collaboration with the Italian manufacturer Cagiva, there is a Senna motorcycle, then a few days before Imola he presented his new mountain bike, produced in collaboration with the Italian firm Carraro... Other projects were planned and the trend was clear: high-tech sports products, jet-skis, as well as personal accessories like watches – and most of them will continue. "But it must all fit the image, it must have high quality – and must therefore be impossible to forge. That's why we don't want to get involved in fashion, for example – too many cheap copies appear too quickly, and you can't do anything about it," said Machado in March 1993.

Yet in April 1994, presented for the first time in Aida, there came an Ayrton Senna collection after all – tee-shirts, sweat-shirts, jackets, "but all the same, not under our official trademark, not as part of the 'Senna' brand with the 'Red S', but as a product made officially under licence in co-operation with an Australian manufacturer." One reason for the change of policy was the realization that in the absence of 'official' Senna products, all kind of things were being forged – for example, in 1993 Senna tee-shirts

A motor yacht – the 'Senna' brand top product.

with the 'S' motif suddenly appeared everywhere. "The official collection is an attempt to keep things at least halfway under control."

In 1993 his cousin Fabio made his assessment of Ayrton Senna as a businessman: "He wants to have an overview of everything. Of course, he doesn't have the time to concern himself with every detail, so it's our job to prepare things properly for him and to give advice. But in the end he makes the decisions himself." Straightforward, very direct, determined, expecting a lot of himself and his colleagues, there is hardly any difference between Senna the businessman and Senna the racing driver. "Because Ayrton is such a strong and straightforward personality he tends to see things only in black and white," smiled Fabio. "Then sometimes I have to step in and find a diplomatic solution."

He remembers the Brazilian Grand Prix of 1993, when Senna's appearance at his home race in Interlagos hung in the balance. "In our contract negotiations with McLaren something had gone wrong, something which he thought had been cleared up but in fact hadn't after all. He got so excited about it that he was ready to throw it all in. Then I had to step in, calm everybody down and get them all to think about the consequences, to look for a solution

– and in the end it worked. It's not always easy to work for Ayrton, but on the other hand I can't imagine a better job."

Fabio is going to continue and has taken on the overall management of the empire with Ayrton's father Milton and Julian Jakobi; practically all the projects will be going ahead and Leonardo will be taking particular responsibility for the continuation of the car business.

"That was always agreed between us," says Jakobi, "I gave this promise to Ayrton: if anything happened to him, then I would stay and we would all continue

together. As he would have wanted." That was the least – and the only thing – that could be done. One thing is particularly important for the family at the moment: "We want at all costs to avoid making a profit out of his death."

Therefore: "All income which comes in any way from projects that are based on Ayrton's image will go to a fund, the 'Ayrton Senna Foundation'. The fund will promote charity projects for children, which Ayrton had earlier supported – mostly anonymously."

Senna's great social involvement, for a long time carried out in strict secrecy in order not to be misunderstood as a PR strategy, is now, perhaps in retrospect, drawing in a wider range of people. Many who were close to him are thinking about what they can do in the future that would be "as he would have wanted". A typical example is his official German fan club, which it has been decided will be kept going, with the primary aim of supporting the fund and "doing something that would have been important to him…"

The man in the background: Julian Jakobi.

"I'm not a machine, you know"

The other side of Ayrton Senna

The gifted racing driver, the pensive philosopher of the race track, the successful buinessman – these public sides of Ayrton Senna are, and always were, more or less well-known. But there was another side, which he allowed only very few people to see, and which belonged to him almost alone.

This was Ayrton Senna, the grown-up child, away from the race track, away from stress and business – happy, fun-loving, carefree...

The big child, who played with his powered model aircraft, most of which he'd built himself: "It's not so easy; above all you need full concentration, otherwise it can happen very quickly that one of them crashes. And when you've built it yourself and know how much work and trouble went into it, then it really hurts." At first, that sort of thing happened to him quite often, but later he mastered his models with great skill – and occasionally he would become highly amused when his cousin Fabio had a lot more trouble with his own planes.

The big child, who loved charging about the area with other children, with his nieces and nephews, whether on water in a

boat, jet-skiing or water-skiing, or driving against his nephew Bruno on his own go-kart track in Tatui: "We really go for it, jostle each other, shove each other off the track, shoot off into the field. I need it for relaxation, to be able to switch off completely, to forget completely Formula 1 with all its stress."

When he was out with the jet-ski at Angra, quite often he would send friends out ahead of him in the motor boat to make a few artificial waves, "so that I can jump over them, so that there's a bit of action."

Speed was what all his leisure activities had to have. Golf, the favourite relaxation of many of his Formula 1 colleagues, held absolutely no attraction for him: "I'm not going to give up four hours of my valuable time for a single game in which nothing happens." He just shook his head when Fabio once tried to persuade him to play when they were on holiday in Port Douglas, between the Japanese and Australian Grands Prix...

But on one occasion he does eventually let himself be persuaded to eat out in a somewhat freaky Australian pub, away from the sheltered hotel world, with just a

small group of five people. At the beginning he is obviously still a bit sceptical, and it takes a little while for him to thaw, but then he enjoys it. He also enjoys not being recognized by anybody for a whole evening in the semi-darkness of the pub – or at least not having anybody come up to speak to him... Of course, this has its downside. The VIP special treatment is absent, a cola ordered without ice comes with ice; he's not quite used to that kind of thing...

But then he joins in the jokes of Alex, the German owner of the place, whom he nicknamed `Viking' almost as soon as he saw him; the attractive waitress gets the name 'Linda' – and the puzzled lady swiftly gets the explanation: "That means pretty" – in Portuguese, of course.

What he particularly likes is the changing background music in *Going Bananas*. He listens to it and takes it in: "I like lots of different types of music – the main thing is that it's good music." When suddenly a Bach chorale is played, he pricks up his ears: "I've never heard anything like that, but it's great, I like it." He even makes something of a rather strange Australian aboriginal song: "You've got to listen carefully – those are the natural sounds of Australia!"

This evening he tells one funny story after another, about some crash or other, and also about the legendary jokes between himself and Gerhard Berger... And he doesn't leave out Portugal, that "end of the European season party of 1992", when he really 'copped it': "I hadn't eaten anything since midday, since before the race, and in the evening we went to this

The 'big child' and his favourite toys: model aeroplanes. ▷

152

disco, and the whisky glasses were going the rounds; everybody wanted to drink a toast with me – and that was it." Just about the entire McLaren team was pretty canned on that Sunday in September 1992, but it's a surprise to many people that something like that could happen to Senna, who would normally drink, at the most, a couple of glasses of champagne when there's a new world title to celebrate. "I just felt awful, it was really bad..." At about 1.30 the following morning Josef Leberer brought him home, "but putting me to bed wasn't a particularly good solution. It's not a nice feeling when you keep on thinking you must hold on to the bed to stop it tipping over with you... Even telling the story he shakes with laughter at the thought...

He can't help it, either, when he thinks of all the things that Gerhard Berger did to him in their three years together at McLaren: "Gerhard can be merciless, you have to expect anything..." On one occasion his expensive, and always immaculately tidy, attaché case was suddenly thrown out of the helicopter at Monza, "and when I cautiously complained, Gerhard just commented: 'If you had a cheap one like I do, you wouldn't need to get so worked up...'" Incidentally, Senna got back his precious case, even if it was slightly damaged...

Once, when the two of them were driving in Milan in a Ferrari, in the thick of the traffic in the middle of a crossroads Gerhard pulled the ignition key out and threw it out of the window. A passing policeman, who wanted to tear a strip off the apparently incompetent Ferrari driver who had stalled his car, went as red as a beetroot when he recognized Senna – and the three of them ended up crawling around in the road looking for the key...

The smelly cheese, dead fish, etc,

hidden in hotel rooms are already legendary, and once in Australia it was even a load of 26 frogs... Senna would usually scream just one word: "Berger!"

His acts of revenge were usually quite harmless by comparison: Berger's hotel room would be turned upside-down, or his racing overalls would suddenly disappear, then turn up on the tarmac in front of the McLaren truck after Gerhard, wearing just his racing under-wear, had been rushing around desperately looking for his gear while Senna watched, laughing to himself in the corner – a scene from Hungary in 1991.

But Ayrton had to be careful: if he ever dared to 'attack' Gerhard, he usually got paid back two or three times over: "The business with the chaos in the hotel room happened in 1991 in Australia, before Adelaide – and what did he do? In Adelaide, he rips pages out of my passport and decorates it instead with a few *Playboy*-type photos... I didn't notice, so when I flew back to Brazil via Argentina there were a few very astonished faces in Passport Control and I had to kick my heels for half an hour..."

Often, Josef Leberer was included in these pranks. "Once, in Monza during the tests, the two of them unbolted all the wheels off my car and placed it on four wooden blocks. I caught them at it..." But Josef knew how to retaliate. "The next day it was my turn to laugh. I thoroughly treated the hire car the two of them had rented together with Japanese herb oil [an incredibly powerful nasal decongestant]... a few drops here, a few there, all spread around nice and evenly. It was hot, and the car stood all day in the sun, so the effect was correspondingly enhanced. When Ayrton and Gerhard got in, it almost knocked them over." Then the two thought

they'd be really clever: "Quick, put the air-conditioning on to get some fresh air." But they hadn't reckoned on Josef: "For in the air-conditioning there was another good squirt of the stuff..."

From being so much in Berger's company Senna learnt something which previously had escaped him: that even in the close environment of Formula 1, even during a Grand Prix weekend, it was possible to let yourself relax a bit from time to time, and that it doesn't have to be

detrimental to your performance, on the contrary...

Then he tried it out on a few others, apart from Berger. On one occasion Ron Dennis was the victim: "We were eating in Mexico; my brother was with us and I know that he likes really hot food. He'd already tried the chili on the table, so I asked him, in Portuguese, so that the others wouldn't understand, how hot it was. `Very,' he said – and if he finds it hot... So I bet Ron $5,000 that he couldn't eat the whole dish. He took a spoon and began, and his face went scarlet – but he ate up the whole dish..."

Recalling the episode long afterwards, he is still amused by the memory, and can describe most vividly how the usually reserved and image-conscious McLaren chief fought with the fire in his throat. Everybody present has a good laugh... And then, at some point, in the midst of this relaxed atmosphere, Ayrton comments, quite pensively: "And people say I'm a machine, that I don't know how to have fun..." His eyes convey the message that it hurts, that he would like people to see him as he really is. But it was only a few who were allowed to experience this side of him...

A lot of fun together: Ayrton Senna and Gerhard Berger, the best of friends in Formula 1.

Goodbye champion, farewell friend!

oodbye, Ayrton. It is difficult to say farewell after having known you for 10 years. It was a decade during which, especially in the final years, we were maybe just a little bit closer than is usual between a Formula 1 world star and one of those ever-disturbing journalists. Years during which I like to think we became friends.

So this is the time to say farewell to a friend, and to say how much those of us who were privileged to get to know you better than most, and as a consequence came to admire you all the more, will miss you, and how long it will be before we are able to understand and accept that you are gone forever.

You knew about this book, and

you knew that I wanted to finish it at the end of 1994, for obvious reasons – we were both convinced that its publication would then coincide with your fourth World Championship. You had promised me your help with it, and of course our many talks together, especially during the last months, have helped me greatly through what has been a painful task. I just hope that you would have been at least halfway content with the outcome, and that you would have recognized yourself through these pages...

Goodbye, Ayrton. It is hard to see someone going who still had so many plans, so many more aims in life. "I want to live long to always improve myself, not only in my racing but in life in general," you told me last winter in Paris during that go-kart meeting, when you were so happy, so relaxed, so full of confidence, with your girlfriend Adriane always beside you.

You hinted to me about some of your future plans, especially *Senninha*, the project that was so important and meant so much to you. When I visited your office in São Paulo, the day after the 1994 Brazilian Grand Prix, you wanted to know everything that had happened concerning *Senninha* during the previous week, and you were on the phone to your project manager about it for about half-an-hour.

You were not one of those people who reach sporting stardom, but fail to recognize anything else in the world beyond

the horizon of their own success. Your home country Brazil was so very important to you, and you were all too aware of the dark sides of it. They worried you a lot, and you tried to help as much as you could. Especially for the children, because you loved children so much; they could get anything from you. I never saw you refusing an autograph to a child, not even during the most difficult and tense moments before the start of a race.

You liked so much to play with your sister's children, and when you

were with them you became a big child again yourself... It is so sad that you never had the chance to have your own family – it was something you wanted so much, "at the right moment", as you used to say, which probably meant only after your racing career was over, when it was no longer necessary to devote 100 per cent of your life to it.

Goodbye, Ayrton. You were so different from what most people thought about you. They called you cool, because they never had the chance to see you in different situations and atmospheres, away from the stressful, hectic Grand Prix weekends. In a racing environment you were able to show only rarely – and even then not to everyone – how sensitive and emotional you really were. Because one thing was always difficult for you: to find the confidence to trust others. Deep inside there was always that fear of being betrayed, of being used...

But I cannot understand why so few people realized the extent to which you were affected by others' misfortune, how much you cared when something really bad happened. I will never forget the tears in your eyes after Martin Donnelly's accident in Spain in 1990, nor the expression on your face and in your eyes on Saturday afternoon at Imola this year when we met as you returned from the circuit and you knew, before any of us did, that Roland Ratzenberger had died...

But your tears of joy will be equally unforgettable. In Japan in 1988, when for the first time you

achieved your great ambition, to win the Formula 1 World Championship. Or your first victory at home, in Brazil in 1991, a victory for which you had been waiting for eight years, the one you had wanted so much and for which, in the end, you had to fight so hard and endure so much pain. When I congratulated you in the McLaren pit, two hours after the race, when there were still hundreds of fans waiting patiently for you out front, there was still so much overwhelming joy in you that you gave me a spontaneous hug. Then there was your joy and pride after Donington in 1993 and that memorable first lap in which you went from fifth to first in a demonstration of car control the like of which we had never ever seen. Donington was the place and the day when the 'magic' legend grew – and, of course, you knew it, and when you were called upon to value your own performance, you called it "a statement of an art". It was indeed.

Individual conversations with you are burned forever in my mind. That occasion in Australia in 1992, on holiday in Port Douglas between the Japanese and the Australian GPs, when you suddenly started to talk about Germany, about Hockenheim, about your testing accident there in 1991. You remembered all the details, and you admitted that you thought you "wouldn't get out of this". You didn't use the word "die", but you meant it. And in this context, you mentioned very carefully, almost as though speaking between the lines, that for you there was something much worse than dying: having, perhaps, to live severely handicapped, not being able to live life fully any more... I thought of this time and time again on that dreadful afternoon in Imola as we all awaited the final confirmation...

And at the end of that very long conversation in January this year, in a very private atmosphere, answering a question about your wishes for 1994, when you said: "If, at the end of this year, I am as happy as I am now, on the business and on the private side, then it will have been a very good year..."

But Ayrton, I cannot get rid of one reflection after this last winter, which was your summer in Brazil: Did you have any feelings deep inside you, any premonitions? The way you pushed your business over the winter, setting up so many new projects, the way you tried to make peace with different people, with whom there had been tensions, some of them for a long time...

The things you said about the way you had reacted to Johnny Cecotto's accident in 1984, admitting your own mistakes; your way of trying to improve the relationship with Michael Schumacher from Brazil this year onwards; your greeting to Alain Prost over the Williams radio during the warm-up at Imola; and that phone-call to Adriane on the Saturday...

But if you really felt something, if you believed in fate, you didn't try to avoid it; you decided to face it, whatever the outcome might be. We can admire you all the more for that, even though at the moment it can provide us with little comfort.

Goodbye, Ayrton. I think you would not want us to cry for you for too long. I think instead you would prefer us to hold you in our memories as someone playing your favourite role – as a glorious winner, perhaps the best racing driver there has ever been, and as a fascinating person who was able to give us so much. It will not be easy, but we will give it a try. We owe you that.

Adeus, grande campeao – adeus, grande amigo. Goodbye, Ayrton, and thank you, thank you for everything! Or, in your mother tongue: "Obrigada por tudo!"

AYRTON SENNA
21.3.1960 – 1.5.1994

Statistics

Ayrton Senna's career

Karting

1973 01.07 First race, Interlagos, 1st
1977 South American Championship, 1st
1978 Brazilian Championship, 1st
South American Championship, 1st
World Karts, Le Mans, 6th
1979 Brazilian Championship, 1st
World Karts, Estoril, 2nd
1980 Brazilian Championship, 1st
World Karts, Nivelles, 2nd
1981 Brazilian Championship, 1st
World Karts, Parma, 4th
1982 World Karts, Kalmar, 14th

Formula Ford 1600 (Van Diemen)

(P&O = P&O Ferries Championship
TT = Townsend-Thoresen Championship
RAC = RAC Championship)

(PP = pole position; FL = fastest lap)

1981
01.03 P&O Brands Hatch, 5th
08.03 TT Thruxton, 3rd
15.03 TT Brands Hatch, 1st
22.03 TT Mallory Park, PP/2nd
05.04 TT Mallory Park, 2nd
03.05 TT Snetterton, PP/2nd
24.05 RAC Oulton Park, FL/1st
25.05 TT Mallory Park, 1st
07.06 TT Snetterton, FL/1st
21.06 RAC Silverstone, 2nd
27.06 TT Oulton Park, FL/1st
04.07 RAC Donington Park, FL/1st
12.07 RAC Brands Hatch, FL/4th
25.07 TT Oulton Park, FL/1st
26.07 RAC Mallory Park, FL/1st
02.08 TT Brands Hatch, 1st
09.08 RAC Snetterton, FL/1st
15.08 TT Donington Park, 1st
31.08 TT Thruxton, PP/FL/1st
29.09 TT Brands Hatch, FL/2nd

RAC Champion; Townsend-Thoresen Champion

Formula Ford 2000 (Rushen Green Racing, Van Diemen)

(PB = Pace British FF2000 Championship
EUR = European FF2000 Championship)

(PP = pole position; FL = fastest lap;
Rtd = retired)

1982
07.03 PB Brands Hatch, PP/FL/1st
27.03 PB Oulton Park, PP/FL/1st
28.03 PB Silverstone, PP/FL/1st
04.04 PB Donington Park, PP/FL/1st
09.04 PB Snetterton, PP/FL/1st
12.04 PB Silverstone, PP/FL/1st
19.04 EUR Zolder, PP/Rtd
02.05 EUR Donington Park, PP/FL/1st
03.05 PB Mallory Park, FL/1st
09.05 EUR Zolder, PP/FL/Rtd
30.05 PB Oulton Park, Rtd
31.05 PB Brands Hatch, FL/1st
06.06 PB Mallory Park, FL/1st
13.06 PB Brands Hatch, PP/1st
20.06 EUR Hockenheim, PP/Rtd
26.06 PB Oulton Park, FL/1st
03.07 EUR Zandvoort, PP/1st
04.07 PB Snetterton, 2nd
10.07 PB Castle Combe, PP/FL/1st
01.08 PB Snetterton, FL/1st
08.08 EUR Hockenheim, PP/FL/1st
15.08 EUR Zeltweg, PP/FL/1st
22.08 EUR Jyllandsring, PP/FL/1st
30.08 PB Thruxton, 1st
05.09 PB Silverstone, FL/1st
12.09 EUR Mondello Park, FL/1st
26.09 PB Brands Hatch, FL/2nd

British Champion; European Champion

Other races:
30.05 Celebrity race, Oulton Park (Talbot-Sunbeam TI), 1st
13.11 Formula 3, Thruxton (Ralt-Toyota), 1st

British Formula 3 Championship (West Surrey Racing, Ralt-Toyota)

(PP = pole position; FL = fastest lap;
DNS = did not start;
Rtd = retired)

1983
06.03 Silverstone, FL/1st
13.03 Thruxton, PP/1st
20.03 Silverstone, PP/FL/1st
27.03 Donington Park, PP/FL/1st
04.04 Thruxton, PP/1st
24.04 Silverstone, PP/FL/1st
02.05 Thruxton, PP/FL/1st
08.05 Brands Hatch, PP/FL/1st
30.05 Silverstone, PP/FL/1st
12.06 Silverstone, Rtd
19.06 Cadwell Park, PP/DNS
03.07 Snetterton, FL/Rtd
16.07 Silverstone, PP/FL/Rtd
24.07 Donington Park, PP/FL/2nd
06.08 Oulton Park, FL/Rtd
29.08 Silverstone, PP/1st

11.09 Oulton Park, Rtd
18.09 Thruxton, PP/Rtd
02.10 Silverstone, 2nd
23.10 Thruxton, PP/FL/1st

British Champion

Other race:
20.10 Formula 3 Macau GP (Teddy Yip, Ralt-Toyota), PP/FL/1st

Formula 1 (Toleman-Hart)

(FL = fastest lap; DNQ = did not qualify; DNS = did not start;
Rtd = retired)

1984
25.03 Brazilian GP, Rio, Rtd
07.04 South African GP, Kyalami, 6th
29.04 Belgian GP, Zolder, 6th
06.05 San Marino GP, Imola, DNQ
20.05 French GP, Dijon, Rtd
03.06 Monaco GP, Monte Carlo, FL/2nd
17.06 Canadian GP, Montreal, 7th
24.06 United States East GP, Detroit, Rtd
08.07 United States GP, Dallas, Rtd
22.07 British GP, Brands Hatch, 3rd
05.08 German GP, Hockenheim, Rtd
19.08 Austrian GP, Zeltweg, Rtd
26.08 Dutch GP, Zandvoort, Rtd
09.09 Italian GP, Monza, DNS
07.10 European GP, Nurburgring, Rtd
21.10 Portuguese GP, Estoril, 3rd

World Championship: 9th, 13 points
World Champion: Niki Lauda (McLaren-TAG Porsche)

Other races:
12.05 Mercedes-Benz 190E-16 inaugural race, 1st
15.07 Nurburgring 1000Kms (Joest Porsche 956), 8th

Formula 1 (Lotus-Renault)

(PP = pole position; FL = fastest lap;
Rtd = retired)

1985
07.04 Brazilian GP, Rio, Rtd
21.04 Portuguese GP, Estoril, PP/FL/1st
05.05 San Marino GP, Imola, PP/7th
19.05 Monaco GP, Monte Carlo, PP/Rtd
16.06 Canadian GP, Montreal, FL/16th
23.06 United States GP, Detroit, PP/FL/Rtd
07.07 French GP, Le Castellet, Rtd
21.07 British GP, Silverstone, 10th
04.08 German GP, Nurburgring, Rtd
18.08 Austrian GP, Zeltweg, 2nd
25.08 Dutch GP, Zandvoort, 3rd
08.09 Italian GP, Monza, PP/3rd
15.09 Belgian GP, Spa-Francorchamps, 1st
06.10 European GP, Brands Hatch, PP/2nd
19.10 South African GP, Kyalami, Rtd
03.11 Australian GP, Adelaide, PP/Rtd

World Championship: 4th, 38 points
World Champion: Alain Prost (McLaren-TAG Porsche)

1986
23.03 Brazilian GP, Rio, PP/2nd
13.04 Spanish GP, Jerez, PP/1st
27.04 San Marino GP, Imola, PP/Rtd
11.05 Monaco GP, Monte Carlo, 3rd
25.05 Belgian GP, Spa-Francorchamps, 2nd
15.06 Canadian GP, Montreal, 5th
22.06 United States GP, Detroit, PP/1st
06.07 French GP, Le Castellet, PP/Rtd
13.07 British GP, Brands Hatch, Rtd
27.07 German GP, Hockenheim, 2nd
10.08 Hungarian GP, Hungaroring, PP/2nd
17.08 Austrian GP, Zeltweg, Rtd
07.09 Italian GP, Monza, Rtd
21.09 Portuguese GP, Estoril, PP/4th
12.10 Mexican GP, Mexico City, PP/3rd
26.10 Australian GP, Adelaide, Rtd

World Championship: 4th, 55 points
World Champion: Alain Prost (McLaren-TAG Porsche)

Formula 1 (Lotus-Honda)

(PP = pole position; FL = fastest lap;
Rtd = retired)

1987
12.04 Brazilian GP, Rio, Rtd
03.05 San Marino GP, Imola, PP/2nd
17.05 Belgian GP, Spa-Francorchamps, Rtd
31.05 Monaco GP, Monte Carlo, FL/1st
21.06 United States GP, Detroit, FL/1st
05.07 French GP, Le Castellet, 4th
12.07 British GP, Silverstone, 3rd
26.07 German GP, Hockenheim, 3rd
09.08 Hungarian GP, Hungaroring, 2nd
16.08 Austrian GP, Zeltweg, 5th
06.09 Italian GP, Monza, FL/2nd
20.09 Portuguese GP, Estoril, 7th
27.09 Spanish GP, Jerez, 5th
18.10 Mexican GP, Mexico City, Rtd
01.11 Japanese GP, Suzuka, 2nd
15.11 Australian GP, Adelaide, Rtd

World Championship: 3rd, 57 points
World Champion: Nelson Piquet (Williams-Honda)

Formula 1 (McLaren-Honda)

(PP = pole position; FL = fastest lap;
Dis = disqualified)

1988
03.04 Brazilian GP, Rio, PP/Dis
01.05 San Marino GP, Imola, PP/1st
15.05 Monaco GP, Monte Carlo, PP/FL/Rtd
29.05 Mexican GP, Mexico City, PP/2nd
12.06 Canadian GP, Montreal, PP/FL/1st

19.06	United States GP, Detroit, PP/1st		
03.07	French GP, Le Castellet, 2nd		
10.07	British GP, Silverstone, 1st		
24.07	German GP, Hockenheim, PP/1st		
08.08	Hungarian GP, Hungaroring, PP/1st		
28.08	Belgian GP, Spa-Francorchamps, PP/1st		
11.09	Italian GP, Monza, PP/Rtd		
25.09	Portuguese GP, Estoril, 6th		
02.10	Spanish GP, Jerez, PP/4th		
30.10	Japanese GP, Suzuka, PP/FL/1st		
13.11	Australian GP, Adelaide, PP/2nd		

World Champion, 90 points

1989

26.03	Brazilian GP, Rio, PP/11th
23.04	San Marino GP, Imola, PP/1st
07.05	Monaco GP, Monte Carlo, PP/1st
28.05	Mexican GP, Mexico City, PP/1st
04.06	United States GP, Phoenix, PP/FL/Rtd
18.06	Canadian GP, Montreal, Rtd
09.07	French GP, Le Castellet, Rtd
16.07	British GP, Silverstone, PP/Rtd
30.07	German GP, Hockenheim, PP/FL/1st
13.08	Hungarian GP, Hungaroring, 2nd
27.08	Belgian GP, Spa-Francorchamps, PP/1st
10.09	Italian GP, Monza, PP/Rtd
24.09	Portuguese GP, Estoril, PP/Rtd
01.10	Spanish GP, Jerez, PP/FL/1st
22.10	Japanese GP, Suzuka, PP/FL/Dis
05.11	Australian GP, Adelaide, PP/Rtd

World Championship: 2nd, 60 points
World Champion: Alain Prost
(McLaren-Honda)

1990

11.03	United States GP, Phoenix, 1st
25.03	Brazilian GP, Interlagos, PP/3rd
13.05	San Marino GP, Imola, PP/Rtd
27.05	Monaco GP, Monte Carlo, PP/FL/1st
10.06	Canadian GP, Montreal, PP/1st
24.06	Mexican GP, Mexico City, 20th
08.07	French GP, Le Castellet, 3rd
15.07	British GP, Silverstone, 3rd
29.07	German GP, Hockenheim, PP/1st
12.08	Hungarian GP, Hungaroring, 2nd
26.08	Belgian GP, Spa-Francorchamps, PP/1st
09.09	Italian GP, Monza, PP/FL/1st
23.09	Portuguese GP, Estoril, 2nd
30.09	Spanish GP, Jerez, PP/Rtd
21.10	Japanese GP, Suzuka, PP/Rtd
04.11	Australian GP, Adelaide, PP/Rtd

World Champion, 78 points

1991

10.03	United States GP, Phoenix, PP/1st
24.03	Brazilian GP, Interlagos, PP/1st
28.04	San Marino GP, Imola, PP/1st
12.05	Monaco GP, Monte Carlo, PP/1st
02.06	Canadian GP, Montreal, Rtd
16.06	Mexican GP, Mexico City, 3rd
07.07	French GP, Magny Cours, 3rd
14.07	British GP, Silverstone, 4th
28.07	German GP, Hockenheim, 7th
11.08	Hungarian GP, Hungaroring, PP/1st

25.08	Belgian GP, Spa-Francorchamps, PP/1st
08.09	Italian GP, Monza, PP/FL/2nd
22.09	Portuguese GP, Estoril, 2nd
29.09	Spanish GP, Barcelona, 5th
20.10	Japanese GP, Suzuka, FL/2nd
03.11	Australian GP, Adelaide, PP/1st

World Champion, 96 points

1992

10.03	South African GP, Kyalami, 3rd
22.03	Mexican GP, Mexico City, Rtd
05.04	Brazilian GP, Interlagos, Rtd
03.05	Spanish GP, Barcelona, 9th
17.05	San Marino GP, Imola, 3rd
31.05	Monaco GP, Monte Carlo, 1st
14.06	Canadian GP, Montreal, PP/Rtd
05.07	French GP, Magny Cours, Rtd
12.07	British GP, Silverstone, Rtd
26.07	German GP, Hockenheim, 2nd
16.08	Hungarian GP, Hungaroring, 1st
30.08	Belgian GP, Spa-Francorchamps, 5th
13.09	Italian GP, Monza, 1st
27.09	Portuguese GP, Estoril, FL/3rd
25.10	Japanese GP, Suzuka, Rtd
08.11	Australian GP, Adelaide, Rtd

World Championship: 4th, 50 points
World Champion: Nigel Mansell
(Williams-Renault)

Formula 1 (McLaren-Ford)

(PP = pole position; Rtd = retired)

1993

14.03	South African GP, Kyalami, 2nd
28.03	Brazilian GP, Interlagos, 1st
11.04	European GP, Donington Park, FL/1st

25.04	San Marino GP, Imola, Rtd
09.05	Spanish GP, Barcelona, 2nd
23.05	Monaco GP, Monte Carlo, 1st
13.06	Canadian GP, Montreal, 18th
04.07	French GP, Magny Cours, 4th
11.07	British GP, Silverstone, 5th
25.07	German GP, Hockenheim, 4th
15.08	Hungarian GP, Hungaroring, Rtd
29.08	Belgian GP, Spa-Francorchamps, 4th
12.09	Italian GP, Monza, Rtd
26.09	Portuguese GP, Estoril, Rtd
24.10	Japanese GP, Suzuka, 1st
07.11	Australian GP, Adelaide, PP/1st

World Championship: 2nd, 73 points
World Champion: Alain Prost
(Williams-Renault)

Formula 1 (Williams-Renault)

(PP = pole position; Rtd = retired)

1994

27.03	Brazilian GP, Interlagos, PP/Rtd
17.04	Pacific GP, Aida, PP/Rtd
01.05	San Marino GP, Imola, PP/fatal accident

Formula 1 record:

Grands Prix contested: 161
Pole positions: 65
Grand Prix victories: 41
Fastest laps: 19
World Championship points: 614
World Championships: 3

Other MRP motorsport books include:

Gilles Villeneuve: The Life of the Legendary Racing Driver/Gerald Donaldson (ISBN 0 947981 44 6)
Champions!: Hawthorn, Hill, Clark, Surtees, Stewart, Hunt, Mansell/Christopher Hilton & John Blunsden (ISBN 0 947981 76 4)
Racers Apart: Memories of Motorsport Heroes/David Tremayne (ISBN 0 947981 58 6)
A Man Called Mike (Hailwood): The Inspiring Story of a Shy Superstar/Christopher Hilton (ISBN 0 947981 92 6)
BRM: The Saga of British Racing Motors Vol 1: The Front-Engined Cars 1945-60/Doug Nye (ISBN 0 947981 37 3)

British Library Cataloguing-in-Publication Data.
A catalogue record for this book is available from the British Library.

Ayrton Senna: Goodbye Champion, Farewell Friend/Karin Sturm
ISBN 0 947981 86 1
First published 1994

MOTOR RACING PUBLICATIONS LTD
Unit 6, The Pilton Estate, 46 Pitlake, Croydon CR0 3RY, England

© 1994 by Sport und Gesundheit Verlag GmbH, Berlin
© 1994 English language edition by Motor Racing Publications Ltd

Cover photographs: ATP (front), Ferdi Krähling (rear)
Text photographs: Lukas Gorys (38): 4/5, 15, 16/17, 19, 26, 31, 46/47, 50, 51, 52/53, 54, 55, 61, 62/63, 69, 71, 72/73, 74/75, 76/77, 78/79, 80, 83, 84, 86/87, 89, 90/91, 94/95, 97, 98/99, 103, 105, 106/107, 116/117, 118/119, 124/125, 127, 128, 132; ATP/Thill (11): 8/9, 40/41, 45, 58/59, 66/67, 80/81, 104, 114/115, 121, 122, 154/155; ATP/Reck (10): 6, 21, 28, 33, 35, 48/49, 60/61, 100/101, 113, 137; ATP/Larkin (4): 2/3, 12, 24/25, 147/148; ATP/DPPI (3): 36, 37; ATP/Kaneko (2): 30, 34; ATP/Stirnberg (1): 102; ATP/Hamann (1): 130/131; ATP/IPA (1): 140/141; ICN UK Bureau (1) 158; Ferdi Kräling (7): 13, 27, 29, 43, 56/57, 110/111, 134/135; Sports News (3): 32, 38/39, 44; ASPL (2): 150, 151; Phoenix GP Office/PR (2): 153, 156/157; Daniel Reinhard (1): 92/93; Jimmy Froideveaux (1): 126; Gerd Krämer (1) 145; Karin Sturm (13): 11, 22, 23, 64/65, 108, 109, 123, 129, 142, 143, 149, 151, 156.

Printed and bound by Offizin Andersen Nexö GmbH, Leipzig